Things Grew Beautifully Worse

Things Grew Beautifully Worse:
The Wartime Experiences of
Captain John O'Brien,
30th Arkansas Infantry, C.S.A.

Things Grew Beautifully Worse:
The Wartime Experiences of
Captain John O'Brien,
30th Arkansas Infantry, C.S.A.

Edited by

Brian K. Robertson

Butler Center for Arkansas Studies
Central Arkansas Library System
2001

O'Brien, John, 1827-1913.
    Things grew beautifully worse: the wartime experiences of Captain
John O'Brien, 30th Arkansas Infantry, C.S.A. / edited by Brian K.
Robertson.
     xx, 68 p. ; 23 cm.---(Butler Center Book Series)
     ISBN 0-9708574-1-1
       1. O'Brien, John, 1827-1913. 2. Confederate States of America.
Army. Arkansas Infantry Regiment, 30th. 3. Confederate States of
America. Army. Arkansas Infantry Regiment, 25th. 4. United States--
History--Civil War, 1861-1865--Personal narratives, Confederate. 5.
Arkansas--History--Civil War, 1861-1865--Personal narratives. I.
Robertson, Brian K., 1971-
E553.5 30th .O27 2001
973.7467 O---dc

Copyright © 2001 by Butler Center for Arkansas Studies

Library of Congress Catalog Card Number: 2001089436
ISBN: 0-9708574-1-1

First published in 2001
First Edition

Butler Center for Arkansas Studies, Central Arkansas Library System, 100 Rock
Street, Little Rock, AR 72201

Printed in the United States of America

The paper used in this book complies with the Permanent Paper Standard issued
by the National Information Standards Organization (Z39.48-1984).

Cover illustration: Battle of Stones River, *copyrighted and published by Kurz & Allison, 1891.*

This volume is dedicated to all Americans
who have made the ultimate sacrifice for freedom.

Contents

Foreword *page xi*

Diary *page 22*

Epilogue *page 50*

Appendix A: Roster *page 53*

Appendix B: Clothing Issuances *page 59*

Appendix C: Food Rations *page 61*

Bibliography *page 63*

About the Editor *page 69*

List of Illustrations

John O'Brien   *page xviii*
Brig. Gen. Evander McNair   *page 5*
Maj. Gen. John P. McCown   *page 5*
Map of the Battle of Murfreesboro (Tennessee)   *page 6*
Camp Morton   *page 19*
Fort Delaware   *page 21*
Map of Johnson's Island   *page 24*
Sketch of Johnson's Island Military Prison   *page 24*
Hoffman Battalion/128th Ohio Volunteer Infantry   *page 29*
Hoffman Battalion/128th Ohio Volunteer Infantry   *page 30*
Confederate Veterans Reunion, 1902   *page 51*
Battle Flag   *page 58*

Foreword

In the spring of 1865 the guns fell silent when Confederate commander Robert E. Lee surrendered to General U. S. Grant. While the guns have been silent now for almost 140 years, the historians have not! No aspect of American history has received the heart-felt attention that researchers have given the "War of the Rebellion." But, in the field of Arkansas civil war history much remains to be done.

It is true that Arkansans through the years have erected the ubiquitous Confederate statue on courthouse lawns throughout the state. What we have not done is systematically comb through our collective attics in search of the original sources that document the war in our state. In part this is due to our lack of a publishing infrastructure in Arkansas; we did not even get a university press until 1980!

Those of us who are working diligently to reclaim our state heritage tend to be optimistic. It is never too late to begin saving our heritage! With that sense of optimism guiding us, the Butler Center has embarked on a program to publish books on Arkansas history. We are especially interested in publishing (or reprinting) short works, and particularly eye-witness accounts.

One reason we so desperately need these eye-witness writings (called "primary sources" by historians) is their role in humanizing our history. History is the story of how humans have interacted through time, how we have shaped our lives, how we have celebrated and mourned, prospered and perished. It might be a story with convoluted twists, but it is still a human story.

The diary we publish in this book is the very human story of one Arkansan and his experiences in America's most tragic war. It is the story of an Irish immigrant who marches off to war, is wounded, and spends the remainder of his service in a series of Union prisoner-of-war camps. But, it is also the story of a father who loves his wife and sons. With him we suffer his physical and emotional pains. We can only marvel at this prisoner's optimism and hope for his adopted Confederate homeland. We are indebted to the Old State House Museum, an agency of the Department of Arkansas Heritage, which holds the original diary and made it available for publication.

The Butler Center invites you to join us in our efforts to document Arkansas history. You can help us by recommending manuscripts for publication, by letting others know of this project, and, most importantly, by *buying our books*. Indeed, book publishing is a very expensive undertaking, and we are seeking partners who will help us build our publishing endowment.

Now, settle back and read this book; let it transport you into the past. Allow this book to serve as a window into our heritage.

Tom W. Dillard
Curator
Butler Center for Arkansas Studies
Central Arkansas Library System

Acknowledgements

I am indebted to a number of individuals who provided invaluable assistance in bringing this book to fruition. First and foremost I am particularly grateful to Tom W. Dillard for giving me the opportunity to transcribe and edit this diary. His confidence in my abilities propelled me to successful completion. A special thanks also goes to Bill Gatewood, Director of the Old State House Museum, for his support in this endeavor.

Jo Ellen Maack, Collections Manager of the Old State House, promptly and eagerly responded to my requests for assistance. Dr. Bobby Roberts and Tom W. Dillard read over the draft manuscript and provided a number of useful suggestions. The Inter-Library Loan Department of the Central Arkansas Library System worked tirelessly to secure a number of valuable resources. Timothy G. Nutt skillfully composed the layout and design of the book.

The following individuals and institutions also gave considerable help: the staff of the Stones River National Battlefield, the Ohio Historical Society, Ellen Rendle of the Historical Society of Delaware, Julia Rather of the Tennessee State Library and Archives, Bryan Howerton, Anthony Rushing, Russell Baker of the Arkansas History Commission, the United States Army Military History Institute, the Kentucky Department for Libraries and Archives, Linda McDowell of the Butler Center for Arkansas Studies, the Columbus, Ohio Metropolitan Library, Randolph County Historical Society, the Franklin County, Ohio Genealogical Society, and Maggie Marconi of the Sandusky, Ohio Public Library.

Finally, I would like to thank my wife, Mari, for her enduring patience and understanding as I labored on this project.

Introduction

John O'Brien was born September 2, 1827, in County Westmeath, Ireland. At the age of twenty he emigrated to the United States. In 1850 he enlisted in the United States Army and became a noncommissioned officer in the cavalry. He served for nearly five years on the frontier from Fort Laramie, Wyoming to the Mexican border. At some point after that, O'Brien moved to New York for he was married to Miss Anne Bohan of Brooklyn on October 12, 1856. On the 24th of October, the newlyweds left New York on the packet ship *Wellington* and headed for Arkansas. They arrived in New Orleans nineteen days later and from there took a steamboat to Napoleon, Arkansas. From that point, it was a two day journey by stage to reach their final destination of Little Rock. After arriving in Little Rock, O'Brien engaged in the mercantile and general contracting business. He was responsible for building many of the early levees in Pulaski County. The O'Briens had their first child, James, in August 1857. A second child, John, Jr., was born January 26, 1859.

As the threat of war was growing, the Capitol Guards, one of Little Rock's local militia companies, reorganized in July 1857. O'Brien was reputedly a charter member. The Capitol Guards was composed of some of Little Rock's most prominent citizens. The unit had originally seen service during the Mexican War. On June 10, 1861 the Capitol Guards were sworn into state service as Co. A of the 6th Arkansas Infantry Regiment. However, because of business obligations, O'Brien was unable to leave with the unit when it departed for service.

After missing his first opportunity to march off to war, O'Brien succeeded in getting another chance when he joined the 8th Arkansas Infantry Battalion on March 15, 1862. The unit was organized in Little Rock, and O'Brien was elected 2nd Lieutenant of Co. C. The company was known for a time as the Peyton Artillery, but it is unknown why their status changed from artilleryman to infantryman. In May, the company, which was under the command of

Captain James J. Franklin, was transferred to Turnbull's 11th Arkansas Infantry Battalion. On June 18, 1862, the unit was designated the 30th Arkansas Infantry Regiment. O'Brien's company became Co. F of the new organization, and he was promoted to the captaincy on June 22. The regiment fought at Richmond, Kentucky on August 29-30, 1862 and was involved in the fighting at Perryville, Kentucky on October 8, 1862. On New Years Eve 1862, the 30th Arkansas was engaged in the Battle of Murfreesboro, Tennessee. O'Brien was wounded in action and subsequently captured. It is interesting to note that on December 12, 1862, only nineteen days before the battle, Captain O'Brien applied for a forty day leave of absence to return to Little Rock and attend his sick wife. Obviously, the request was denied, but it provides for interesting speculation as to how O'Brien's life would have turned out had it been granted. Shortly after the Battle of Murfreesboro, the 30th Arkansas was renumbered, and it became known as the 25th Arkansas Infantry Regiment.

Brian K. Robertson

Editor's Methodology

Captain John O'Brien began writing his diary while a prisoner following his capture at Murfreesboro, Tennessee. The diary is pocket-sized, measuring approximately four by six inches and is about 100 pages in length. I have tried not to infringe upon O'Brien's original text and have made only those changes necessary for the sake of readability. For the most part I have left O'Brien's spelling intact. Words that were misspelled but easily decipherable have been left alone, while words that are less clear have been corrected. In the case of abbreviations I have followed the same rule and retained only those that are readily distinguishable. Any substantial additions to the text have been placed in brackets. I have also regularized capitalization throughout the text. Punctuation was virtually non-existent in the manuscript so I have added enough to facilitate comprehension. The dates at the top of the pages were not O'Brien's, but have been added for clarification.

John O'Brien, ca. 1860.
Courtesy: Old State House Museum, an agency of the Department of Arkansas Heritage

The following incidents of my prison life I've written for two reasons. The first is that it helps to amuse me hearafter and be a sort of memando. The second is that it helped to pass away time during my captivity, but as a great part of the time I was not able to write. Therefore, most of it is pened from memory and dates may not be strictly correct, and when I did get able to write I had to do it in a crowded room amidst confusion, [interruption] and noise. Consequently its not so well done as I could wish, and if any person gets hold of it I beg they wont critisise the spelling or the grammer to closely.

John O'Brien

*A*bout midnight on Friday the 26th Dec 1862 the camps of McCowans Div near Readyville, Tenn got the command to turn out.[1] After a while the troops was ordered to quarters again and told to be ready at a moments notice. At about two oclock [a.m.] they were again ordered to fall in and we took up our line of march for Murfreesboro distant about fourteen miles. The night was very dark and recent heavy rains rendered the roads awlful muddy so that our march was very [fatiguing]. We reached Murfreesboro about 9 oclock [a.m.] and marched out on the Lebanon pike one mile from town. It rained incesantly all the time.[2] We staid hear untill Monday morning [Dec. 29] and owing to the bad state of the roads our waggons did not reach us until we were ordered to change our position so that as far as comisaries stores was concerned we

---

[1]Major General John P. McCown's Division was composed of three brigades with a total effective force of about 4,000 men. The First Brigade composed solely of Texans was commanded by Brigadier General Matthew Duncan Ector. The Second Brigade commanded by James E. Rains was a mixture of troops from Georgia, North Carolina, Tennessee, and Alabama. The Third Brigade was an Arkansas unit under the command of Brigadier General Evander McNair. *The War of the Rebellion: A Compilation of the Official Records of the Union and Confederate Armies*, 70 vols. in 128 books and index (Washington: Government Printing Office, 1880-1901), series I, vol. 20, pt. 1, 660, 911 (cited hereafter as *OR*, and, unless otherwise indicated, all references are to Series I).

[2]The Union Fourteenth Army Corps, shortly to become known as the Army of the Cumberland, had left Nashville at 6:00 a.m. and was heading south. The dilatory Major General William S. Rosecrans finally decided that he was ready to take the offensive. Rosecrans had received a great deal of admonishment from Washington over his seeming lack of progress and initiative. Union fortunes were looking particularly bleak at this time. General Lee had recently given the Federal Army a bloody beating at Fredericksburg. In the deep South, Grant was hard pressed dealing with the Rebel bastion of Vicksburg. His subordinate, William Tecumsah Sherman, had met a bloody repulse at Chickasaw Bluffs. The northern war effort was floundering and President Lincoln was anxious. With "the government demands action" ringing in his ears and the threat of dismissal hanging over his head, Rosecrans decided it was time to move. Confederate General Braxton Bragg had not expected a winter campaign from the Federal troops and had

were indifferently supplied. On Monday [Dec. 29] we were changed to the left of our line.[3] Monday evening and night were exceedingly cold and we suffered much on that account.[4] We staid there all day Tuesday [Dec. 30]. We then thought and were told by Brig. Genrl McNair that we were to be held in reserve, but about noon the skirmishing comenced on our right and gradually approached our position.[5]

---

settled cozily into the countryside around Murfreesboro. The movement by Rosecrans forced Bragg to reposition his widely scattered forces. McCown's division was placed east of Stones River and was to act as the reserve of the Army of Tennessee. At this point Bragg was unsure of the exact point of attack. In addition, his subordinates were not particularly pleased with his chosen line of defense. Lieutenant General William J. Hardee commented, "The field of battle offered no peculiar advantages for defense. The open fields beyond the town are fringed with deep cedar brakes, offering excellent shelter for approaching infantry, and are almost impervious to artillery. The country on every side is entirely open, and. . . accessible to the enemy." Bragg's army was divided by a river which further compounded the problem. Normally the river was fordable in several places, but a strong rainstorm threatened to turn it into an "impassable torrent." Peter Cozzens, *No Better Place to Die: The Battle of Stones River* (Urbana: University of Illinois Press, 1991), 26, 45; *OR*, vol. 20, pt. 1, 184, 911; vol. 20, pt. 2, 117-18.

[3]On December 29, McCown's division moved to the extreme left of the Confederate line. The division was to be placed in position between Lieutenant-General Polk's left and the Triune Road. However, they were unable to find a gap and positioned themselves on the left (south) of the Triune Road. McCown's command occupied the ground 150 yards in front of Polk's advance line. McNair's brigade, Humphreys' Arkansas battery and Douglas' Texas battery, were placed in reserve while McDuffie's Eufaula Light Artillery was in line in support of Rains' brigade. *OR*, vol. 20, pt.1, 911, 925.

[4]Capt. John W. Lavender of the 4th Ark commented, "We had no wood to make fires. We was wet and a cold north wind Blowing, no shelter of timber or any thing Else. Things seemed Desperate. . .We could not Lay down as the ground was wet and muddy and we was very short of Blankets. So we put in a fearful night." Ted R. Worley, ed., *They Never Came Back: The War Memoirs of Captain John W. Lavender, C.S.A.* (Pine Bluff, AR: The Southern Press, 1956), 37-38.

[5]Evander McNair was born near Laurel Hill, North Carolina, April 15, 1820. The following year his family moved to Mississippi and eventually settled in Simpson County. As a young man McNair worked as a merchant in Jackson. During the Mexican War he served in Company E, 1st Mississippi Rifles. His regiment was commanded by Jefferson Davis. In 1856 he moved to Washington, Arkansas and continued in the mercantile business. In 1861 he was elected colonel of the 4th Arkansas Infantry, and fought with Ben McCulloch at Wilson's Creek and Pea Ridge. He also played a conspicuous part in the battle of Richmond, Kentucky. After Murfreesboro he was part of Joseph E. Johnston's effort to relieve Vicksburg. McNair was wounded at Chickamauga and thereafter assigned to the Trans-Mississippi Department. He later took part in Price's Missouri Raid. After the war he moved to New Orleans before eventually returning to Mississippi.

Robinsons Battery (a splendid one) was posted on our right and replied vigourlously to one of the enemys that was anoying our line.[6] The 154th Ten supported it for near two hours.[7] They thundered away at each other. Mean while the musketry on our right kept up a warm and continous fire. The shells from the enemy battery began to tell on our line and several were wounded whilst some fiew were killed. At this time the battery of the Texas Brigade took position in front of our line and began to fire on the enemy.[8] This drew the fire of another of the enemy's batteries on our line which done us considerable harm. About this time one of the casons in Robinsons Battery blew up with a terrific crash, and evening closing in, both of the batteries drew off much to our relief. For no matter how cool and brave troops may be when engaged, its quite another thing to keep them standing in line of battle under a heavy fire of artilary without a chance to reply.

McNair died in Hattiesburg November 13, 1902, and is buried in Magnolia, Mississippi. Ezra J. Warner, *General in Gray: Lives of the Confederate Commanders* (Baton Rouge: Louisiana State University Press, 1959), 205-6.

[6]O'Brien is referring to Felix H. Robertson's battery. The battery was organized on December 21, 1861, at Pensacola, Florida. It was composed of men from Alabama and Florida and armed with six 12 lb. Napoleon cannon. Robertson's battery would suffer twenty casualties during the fighting at Murfreesboro. Stewart Sifakis, *Compendium of the Confederate Armies: Alabama* (New York: Facts on File, 1992), 26; *OR*, vol. 20, pt. 1, 677.

[7]The 154th (Senior)Tennessee Infantry Regiment was actually a prewar militia unit, organized in 1842. With the outbreak of the Civil War they reorganized May 14, 1861, at Randolph, Shelby County. The regiment received permission to use the designation "Senior" to show they predated regiments with lower numbers. The regiment transferred to Confederate service on August 13, 1861, at New Madrid, Missouri. At one point during this particular skirmish, Union troops threatened to charge Robertson's Battery, and the 154th rushed past the guns to meet the attackers. The Union forces then fell back. The regiment went into battle with 245 men and suffered 100 casualties. Thomas A. Wigginton, et al., *Tennesseans in the Civil War* (Nashville: Civil War Centennial Commission, 1964), I, 308-10; *OR*, vol. 20, pt. 1, 748-49.

[8]O'Brien is mistaken in his identification of this unit. This battery is actually Eufaula's Light Artillery. The Alabama Eufaula Battery was organized and mustered into service at Eufuala, Alabama on February 26, 1862. Lieutenant W.A. McDuffie commanded the battery at Murfreesboro. In this particular encounter, the battery did "great damage to one of the enemy's batteries, forcing it to change position, and, prisoners state, dismounting one gun and killing several cannoneers." The battery of the Texas Brigade, Douglas' Battery, was not engaged on this day. *OR*, vol. 20, pt. 1, 925, 943; Sifakis, ed., *Compendium of the Confederate Armies: Alabama*, 12; Lucia Rutherford Douglas, *Douglas's Texas Battery, CSA* (Tyler, TX: Smith County Historical Society, 1966), 56.

After dark we were marched closer to the yankey lines.[9] The cold was intolerable and Genrl McNair told us if we wished to run the risk we could light fires. We did run the risk and kept warm all night and was not molested.[10] A little before daylight he (McNair) sent to the brigade a barrel of whiskey. We all took a good drink of which we stood much inneed and voted McNair the best of Genrls. Just then the order came to "fall in" a word full of meaning to the soldier. At the same time Adjt Genrl Foote[11] came dashing along the line and said to us, "Boys load! You are in for it, Claiborn supports you."[12]

---

[9]Late in the afternoon General Hardee received orders to take command of McCown's division. He moved Cleburne's division from the extreme right of the Confederate line in behind McCown's division. The Confederate front line was now only about 600 or 800 yards from the enemy. Cleburne formed a second line 500 yards behind McCown. *OR*, vol. 20, pt. 1, 773, 912.

[10]Washington L. Gammage, surgeon for the 4th Arkansas, also tried to keep warm, "I got between two rocks, in the bushes, built me a fire, and in company with ten or twelve men, spread my blanket for sleep." Washington Lafayette Gammage, *The Camp, The Bivouac, and the Battlefield; being a History of the Fourth Arkansas Regiment, from Its First Organization down to the Present Date: Its Campaigns and Its Battles, with an Occasional Reference to the Current Events of the Times, including Biographical Sketches of Its Field Officers and Others of the "Old Brigade." The Whole Interspersed Here and There with Descriptions of the Scenery, Incidents of Camp Life, Etc.* (Selma, AL: Cooper & Kimball, 1864), 70.

[11]Captain R.E. Foote was the Assistant Adjutant General of the Third Brigade, McCown's Divison. *OR*, vol. 20, pt. 1, 949.

[12]Major General Patrick Ronayne Cleburne was born March 17, 1828, near Cork, Ireland. He served three years in the British Army before emigrating to the United States in 1849. Cleburne soon moved to Helena, Arkansas and became a partner in a drugstore. He went on to study law and had a successful business prior to the Civil War. With the outbreak of hostilities, he was elected colonel of the 15th Arkansas and then promoted to brigadier general on March 4, 1862. Cleburne's star rose rapidly as he distinguished himself as a superb combat officer. He led a brigade at Shiloh and Perryville and a division at Richmond. He was promoted to major general on December 13, 1862. At Murfreesboro, Cleburne was commended "for the valor, skill, and ability displayed. . . throughout the engagement." The end of the Chattanooga campaign brought Cleburne a vote of thanks from the Confederate Congress for saving the wagon trains of the Army of Tennessee, but he came under a great deal of criticism in the beginning of 1864 for his proposal to free the slaves and arm those willing to fight for the South. Cleburne and his division fought well against overwhelming odds throughout the Atlanta campaign. He was killed in the debacle at Franklin, Tennessee on November 30, 1864. The death of Cleburne possibly ranks second only after the demise of Stonewall Jackson as the most disastrous individual loss for the Confederacy. Warner, *Generals in Gray*, 53-54; *OR*, vol. 20, pt. 1, 670; Craig L. Symonds, *Stonewall of the West: Patrick Cleburne and the Civil War* (Lawrence: University Press of Kansas, 1997), 187.

Brig. Gen. Evander McNair.
*Courtesy: Butler Center for
Arkansas Studies,
Central Arkansas Library System.*

Maj. Gen. John P. McCown.
From: Photographic History of the
Civil War. Edited by Francis Trevelyan
Miller (New York: Review of Reviews
Co., 1911).

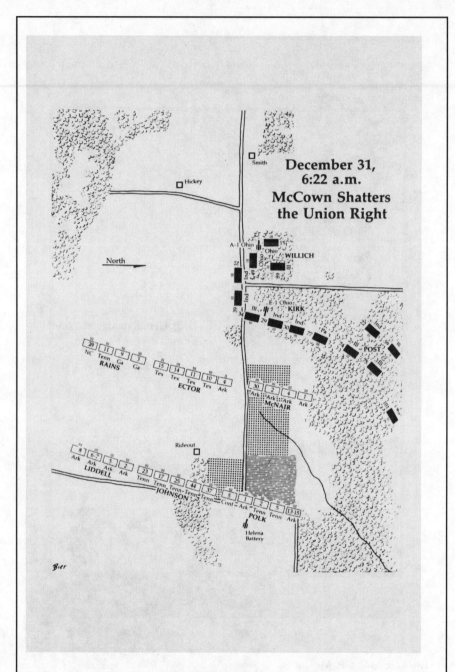

Map of the Battle of Murfreesboro (Tennessee).

From: No Better Place to Die: The Battle of Stones River. *Copyright 1990 by the Board of Trustees of the University of Illinois. Used with permission of the University of Illinois Press.*

This announcement was responded to with a surpressed cheer for the close proximity of the yankeys would not permit of loud demonstrations as our object was to surprise them. As soon as the men got their guns loaded which they done quickly, we were ordered forward.[13]   The enemy's pickets could not be more than six hundred yards in front of us. We moved on without any scirmishers and in five minutes we were on to them. Ross' Battalion first opened fire, the yankeys being in a little point of woods that jutted out towards our line.[14]   In a moment a volley burst from our whole line, and with that terrible yell so charestic of our boys, we rushed at them. The poor yanks were completely bewildered and after a feeble resistance they fell back in disorder.[15]   In their rear was a dense wood of cedars. In this they formed and as we approached they opened a heavy and distinctive fire on us whilst we could not see one of them. Our first dash at them had somewhat disaranged our line, some of it having come in contact with large fences the enemy had thrown together for a sort of breastwork. The yankeys all this time were firing

---

[13]McNair's Brigade was composed of the 1st Arkansas Mounted Rifles, 2nd Arkansas Mounted Rifles, 4th Arkansas, 30th Arkansas, and 4th Arkansas Battalion. At 6:00 a.m. the brigade moved 150 yards forward and joined General Ector's Brigade on the right. They then advanced upon the enemy. *OR*, vol. 20, pt. 1, 944.

[14]Major Jesse A. Ross was the commander of the 4th Arkansas Battalion. The battalion was organized with five companies on November 30, 1861, by Francis A. Terry, a planter and state senator from Little Rock. One company was detached and subsequently served in the heavy artillery. The artillery company was captured at Island No. 10, but the rest of the battalion escaped by wading through the overflow and boarding the transport *Jeff Davis*. After parole the artillery company was sent to Vicksburg and ultimately surrendered with the garrison. Before Murfreesboro, the battalion fought in the Corinth Campaign and at Richmond, Kentucky. They would suffer twenty-nine casualties in this battle. Sifakis, *Compendium of the Confederate Armies: Florida and Arkansas*, 75-76; *OR*, vol. 20, pt. 1, 681; Clement A. Evans, *Confederate Military History: A Library of Confederate States History*, Vol. 10, *Louisiana and Arkansas* (Atlanta: Confederate Publishing Company, 1899), 288-89.

[15]At 6:22 a.m. the Confederates smashed into the right flank of the Union Army. According to Union Brigadier General Edward N. Kirk the Rebels, ". . . moved up steadily, in good order, without music or noise of any kind. They had no artillery in sight." A contemporary historian said, "They poured across the valley in mighty force, swept away the strong line of skirmishers as if they had been cobwebs, and fell upon Kirk's lines like wild beasts." The Union right wing, commanded by Major General Alexander McCook was unprepared for the Confederate onslaught. Several of the field commanders were away from their posts. In addition, though only a short distance separated the two armies, the Union commanders had failed to have all of their troops ready for a possible attack. In fact, many of them were just waking up and eating breakfast. Rifles were stacked and unloaded. It was eerily reminiscent of the surprise attack endured by the Federals at

on us from the cedars and doing considerable harm. At this moment Genrl McNair came dashing allong the line and told us to charge the cedars. Our men again raised their fearful yell and headlong amidst a shower of shell shot and minnie balls they made for the cedars.[16] The yank's again broke cover, but several of their number staid behind, some killed, some wounded, and a great many captured. We also took a splendid battery at this place.[17] But alas for the chances of war just at this moment an unlucky minnie ball struck me just below the right knee ranging downward and to the rear coming out near the ancle.[18]

Shiloh. General Kirk's brigade bore the brunt of the initial Rebel attack. In a foolhardy effort to check or at least slow the Confederate blitz, Kirk ordered the 34th Illinois forward to meet the Rebel line. The incoming fire reminded the sergeant-major of the 34th Illinois "of the passage of a swarm of bees" as the "air. . .seethed with the zip of bullets and grape shot over our heads." The Illinoisans managed one volley against the advancing Confederates which "had no more effect than if they had fired against a stone wall." A few minutes and over 100 casualties later the regiment was ordered to withdraw. The Southerners kept moving. It is ironic that Rosecrans and Bragg had developed almost identical battle plans. Each general planned to have his right wing hold the enemy's left wing in position, while the left wing would assault the other's right. Unfortunately for Rosecrans, Bragg struck first. Cozzens, *No Better Place to Die*, 82-83; Alexander F. Stevenson, *The Battle of Stone's River Near Murfreesboro,Tenn., December 30, 1862 To January 3, 1863* (Boston: James R. Osgood and Company, 1884), 38; William Denison Bickham, *Rosecrans' Campaign with the Fourteenth Army Corps of the Army of the Cumberland: A Narrative of Personal Observations with. . .Official Reports of the Battle of Stone River* (Cincinnati: Moore, Wilstach, Keys & Co., 1863), 228; *OR*, vol. 20, pt. 1, 325; Lyman S. Widney Diary, Stones River National Battlefield; *Northern Indianian*, 4 March 1875, 1.

[16]The dazed Federals were unable to halt the Confederate onslaught. "The rebels. . . ran towards the battery with such a yell that it seemed as though the demons of the lower regions had been let loose." Stevenson, *The Battle of Stone's River Near Murfreesboro, Tenn., December 30, 1862 To January 3, 1863*, 38.

[17]The Confederate troops captured Battery E, First Ohio Light Artillery. The battery's commander, Captain Warren P. Edgarton had sent half of his horses to a small stream approximately 100 rods in his rear to get water and the animals had just reached the stream when the Confederates attacked. Edgarton and his men put up a short, but valiant fight. He described the assault as "fierce" and "overwhelming". At least two of the cannoneers were bayoneted at their guns. Some of the artilleryman fought off their attackers with their swabs. The battery had three men killed, twenty-five wounded and twenty-two, including the captain, taken prisoner. As the Confederate tsunami swept forward, the other units of Kirk's brigade were just as impotent. The shattered brigade literally disintegrated within minutes. Kirk was wounded and captured. *OR*, vol. 20, pt. 1, 300-2; Bickham, *Rosecrans' Campaign with the Fourteenth Army Corps of the Army of the Cumberland: A Narrative of Personal Observations with . . .Official Reports of the Battle of Stone River*, 229; John Fitch, *Annals of the Army of the Cumberland:*

This of course stoped me effectively. For a moment I was undecided how to act, but I said not a word. The line continued to advance and I becoming faint could no longer stand and I sank uppon the field amongst the dead and dying. After a few moments corpl James O. Page of my Co came running up.[19] He seen me and made for me. He kindly assisted me to get up and positively refused to leave me untill he'd see me cared for. With his asistance I reached a large oak a little in our rear. After getting hear I became very faint from loss of blood. Page became very alarmed and expressed his sympathies in a thousand ways. After some trouble he succeeded in finding Dr. Wall's, Ast Surgeon of our Regt.[20] The Dr. hastened to me, bound my wound and told me to lie off good there. That my wound althou painful was by no means a dangerous one. At this entilegence Page expressed his delight. After being repeat-

---

Comprising Biographies, Descriptions of Departments, Accounts of Expeditions, Skirmishes, and Battles; Also Its Police Record of Spies, Smugglers, and Prominent Rebel Emissaries. Together with Anecdotes, Incidents, Poetry, Reminiscences, etc. And Official Reports of the Battle of Stone River and of the Chickamauga Campaign (Philadelphia: J.B. Lippincott and Co., 1864), 394.

[18]The 30th Arkansas had seven of ten company commanders, several lieutenants, and the color bearer cut down in this initial assault. Shortly after Edgarton's battery was captured, the 77th Pennsylvania counterattacked the position. It is unclear as to whether O'Brien was wounded in the charge on the battery or in the counterattack. *OR*, vol. 20, pt. 1, 323, 335, 953; John Obreiter, *The Seventy-Seventh Pennsylvania at Shiloh: History of the Regiment* (Harrisburg, PA: Harrisburg Publishing Company, 1905), 105.

[19]James O. Page was born in Alabama about 1835. The 1860 census lists him as a laborer in Little Rock. His wife, Mary, was born in Canada and they had two children. Page enlisted March 15, 1862 in Little Rock and was appointed corporal December 7, 1862. During the spring of 1863 he was promoted to sergeant. Compiled Service Records of Confederate Soldiers Who Served in Organizations from the State of Arkansas, National Archives Microcopy 317, Roll 187 (cited hereafter as Service Records).

[20]Albert Milton Walls was born February 21, 1832, in Madison County, Alabama. He was educated at Emory and Henry College in Virginia from which he graduated in 1854. Walls went on to graduate from the New Orleans School of Medicine in 1857. He returned to Alabama where he practiced medicine, and in the spring of 1860 moved to Monroe County, Arkansas and set up a private practice. Dr. Walls enlisted March 10, 1862, at Jacksonport as a private; eight days later he was detailed as a hospital steward. Walls was appointed assistant surgeon in July 1862. During the battle in his zeal to do his duty Dr. Walls strayed into the enemy lines and was momentarily captured. However, he was immediately released with advice from the enemy to "not let his zeal outrun his discretion again." He is listed as "present" through the muster roll dated August 1864, at Jonesboro, Georgia. Dr. Walls died in 1869 and is buried at Macedonia Cemetery in Monroe County. Service Records, Roll 188; Gammage, *The Camp, The Bivouac and The Battlefield*, 142-43; Rena Marie Knight, *Confederate Soldiers Buried in Arkansas* (Jacksonville, AR: R.M.K. Publishing Co., 1999), 307.

edly asurded by the surgeon that I was all right, he picked up his musket and with a fond good bye and an injunction to me to take care of myself (which injunction I promised to comply with altho for the life of me I could not see how I was able to do it indeed my ability to take care of myself was any but promising) he hurried on to join his comrades. There is in the army a class of men who make it a point to always try and get to the rear under pretense of attending to the wounded and I seen that Page was afraid that any stigma of that sort would attatch itself to him. I felt relived when I seen him take up the double quick and make for the front and to his credit and honour I record it a better and braver soldier than James O. Page I never met. After a little the Dr. left me to attend to his duties and I was left allone. Then for the first time since we left our bivowac before light that morning I had time for reflection, and I did reflect aye, and what were my reflections. I thought of many things. I at first felt grateful and thanked devine providence that it was no worse. I might have been killed and called away unprepared to meet my maker. I thought of home, of my wife, of my children, of my sister, of all that loved me, of all that was dear to me, but ever and uppermost in my mind was my Dear Dear children. Perhaps at that moment they were speaking of me. Then I thought of their mother again, kind gentle and confiding. What were they all saying and doing at that moment? How long was I going to be laid up with my wound? Wonder if I'd be lame? These and many other such thoughts passed rapidly through my brain. Sometimes it appeared as if it were a terible dream. The loss of rest for several nights, the excitement and noise of the battle, combined with loss of blood, all rendered me incapable of connecting ideas and I lay there in a state of stupor and bewilderment. All this time the infirmary corps never made their appearance. Our division had driven the enemy a long ways.[21] I could tell by the distant report of our guns which kept getting further and further off all the time. Around me lay in all forms and atitudes the dead and wounded, the principal part of which were yankeys. I

---

[21]The impracticality of Bragg's plan now began to show itself. To be successful, the plan called for perfect execution in the movement of his forces, but the wheeling motion envisioned by him was nearly impossible to implement on the battlefield. While some of the troops could move at a walk, others had to run in order to keep the lines formed. The distance to be covered by his troops and terrain were decidedly against him. In addition, the plan did not take into account the fluid nature of battle. While McCown was successful in driving the brigades of Kirk and Willich, he unwittingly allowed his division to be pulled off course. In chasing after the fleeing Federals, his troops were actually being drawn away from the battlefield. Cozzens, *No Better Place to Die*, 89-91.

saw but very few of our men. The enemy suffered most as they retreated in disorder over this ground.[22] I began to wonder with a sort of confused wonder how long I'd have to remain hear when I thought I heard a bugle sound close behind me. I listened and in an instant I heard a discharge of musketry. This roused me up and alarmed me for I knew there were none of our troops in the direction this firing came from. The bugle again sounded and again I heard the discharge of small arms. With the aid of my saber I got up from the ground and strove to hobble off. I hopped a fiew steps when again the fire was repeated behind me and I could distinctly see the leaves on the ground pop all around me as the bullets struck them. This was a critical position. I knew if I continued to go on I ran the risk of getting shot again. I also knew if I turned back to get to the tree my chances were equally bad. But I must do something as it was certain death to stand where I was. So I chose the latter plan, and and well for me I did, so for I had scarcely reached the tree when a volley burst from the yanks which fell thick and fast all around me scalping the bark of my tree in several places. So far I had not seen the parties that were firing. After this last volley I ventured to look round my tree in the direction they were firing from. Close to me I seen a large squad of yankeys under the command of an officer. Our division had driven their right so far that their centre threw this party as flankers to harrass our reserves, but they fired indiscrimanately on our wounded and litter beares.[23] Just as I seen them, three of them made for the tree I was under and one said with an oath, "I have you now, you D—d Rebble." I replied, "Yes, I am your prisoner." He said he did not want any prisoners but that he'd fix me and proceeded deliberately to load his gun. I asked him what he meant. He told me it was none of my business and to keep my D—d head still. He was going to blow it off. I asked him if it was customary in their army to shoot wounded men. Again he told me to dry up. I seen it was useless to talk to him, so I looked at one of his

---

[22]In about thirty minutes McCown's men managed to capture almost 1,000 prisoners and eight pieces of artillery. The Union losses had indeed been heavy. Colonel Joseph B. Dodge, who commanded the second brigade after General Kirk was seriously wounded, was only able to rally about 500 men out of a brigade that numbered almost 2,000 a short time earlier. General August Willich, commander of the first brigade of the second division of the Federal right wing, was captured and his brigade suffered a "severe loss in officers and men". *OR*, vol. 20, pt. 1, 306, 321; Cozzens, *No Better Place to Die*, 88.

[23]In his after action report, General McNair mentions Federal sharpshooters firing upon his wounded. At this discovery he halted his brigade and "moved them to the rear by the flank" in order to protect his wounded. *OR*, vol. 20, pt. 1, 944.

companions. He understood me and told me not to mind him, but he raised his gun and was about to place the musell of it against my head when both companions enterfered and saved my life. Of course I felt grateful that my life was spared. They continued to fire over my head for some time and every time this fellow would load I'd feel uneasy untill he'd again discharge it. In the meantime there was a little scattering fire from some of our men, but I could not see those that were delivering it. Perhaps it was our wounded lying consealed for our supports had not yet come up. How long this painful suspense might last I cannot say, but an occurance took place which quickly relieved me of their presence. Away accross the field as far as the eye could reach and towards the left of where our line had been I seen a section of artilary gallop rapidly into position. The yanks seen it to for their bugle sounded and away they scampered much faster than they came, but as fast as they were the artilary was fast enough for them and Bang Bang went several shots in rapid succession close on their heels. At first I felt greatly relieved at the scamp been driven off, but the artilary continued to fire and I thought they realy made my tree their target. They shot very low and every shot covered me with rotten branches that the shock knocked out of the tree. There was an old fence running parallel with the tree and they made the rails fly in all directions. I thought every minute would be my last as the shells burst in rapid succesion all round me. How I wished they would cease firing. At this juncture I thought I heard some one giving comands. I looked in the derection our supports ought to come and sure enough there came the gallant Patt Claibourne with his Div.[24] They moved up in good order and wounded and

---

[24]As a result of McCown's drift out of the Confederate battle line, Cleburne's division became the forward unit of the Confederate left wing. Cleburne later wrote in his report, ". . .the enemy's skirmishers opened fire along the right and left center of my division, indicating that instead of being a second line supporting McCown's division, I was, in reality, the foremost line on this part of the field, and that McCown's line had unaccountably disappeared from my front." McNair's brigade, which had earlier begun to fall back, soon met up with General Liddell's Arkansas brigade of Cleburne's division. Following some discourse the generals agreed to jointly attack the Union line in their front that was positioned behind a rail fence. After much difficulty and with great loss, the Arkansans managed to drive the Federals back. McCown's costly error combined with his acrimonious relationship with General Bragg resulted in him having no important command after Murfreesboro. In 1868 he moved to a farm near Magnolia, Arkansas. He died January 22, 1879, in Little Rock while attending a meeting of the Grand Lodges of Masons and Odd Fellows. *OR*, vol. 20, pt. 1, 844-45, 944-45; Nathaniel Cheairs Hughes, Jr., ed., *Liddell's Record* (Baton Rouge: Louisiana State University Press, 1997), 108; Cozzens, *No Better Place to Die*, 94; Nettie Hicks Killgore, *History of Columbia County, Arkansas* (Magnolia, AR: Magnolia Printing Co., 1947), 146-47; *Arkansas Democrat*, 22 January 1879.

wary as I was, I felt proud of the fact that I was a soldier and batling in the same cause with them gallant fellows. I also felt a glow of pride rush through my veins as I saw the brave and gallant Claibourne manage his splendid Div. For althou personally a stranger to him I knew he was a true son of the Emerald Isl. Besides, I seen him at Richmond, Ky and I knew what ever he done he done it well.[25] As they moved up, the artilary ceased and I seen two litter bearers coming. I called to them and they came to me. They belonged to the Texas Brigade our Div. They kindly took me on their litter and carried [me] to where there wounded was kept. Hear I found some men of my Regt who took me to where our wounded was being cared for. What a spectale presented itself hear. Men wounded and mangled in the most horrible manner. Piles of legs and arms lay scattered in all directions and several just in the act of dying. Hear I learned for the first time that our Regt suffered severely. Capts Hammond,[26] Black,[27] and Thomas[28] were killed. Whilst Capts Addams,[29]

---

[25]On the morning of August 30, 1862, Confederate forces under the command of General Kirby Smith attacked the Federals at Richmond, Kentucky. Although Cleburne received a painful wound in the mouth, the Rebels were able to carry the day. The Federals suffered a loss of 5,353 out of 6,500, most being captured. Confederate casualties were only 451. The Southerners also managed to capture a large quantity of much needed weapons and supplies. *OR*, vol 16, pt. 1, 936-37, 946.

[26]Richard P. Hammond was born in Georgia and was 42 years old when elected 1st Lieutenant of Co. B in February 1862. He was later promoted to Captain on May 8, 1862. Hammond had seen prior military service during the Mexican War. In that conflict, he served as a sergeant in the Arkansas Regiment of Mounted Volunteers. The 1860 census identifies him as a school teacher from Saline County. He and his wife, Elizabeth, had four sons. Service Records, Roll 186; Desmond Walls Allen, *Arkansas' Mexican War Soldiers* (Conway, AR: Arkansas Research, 1988), 75.

[27]S. Thomas Black joined for duty at Pocahontas and was elected 2nd Lieutenant of Co. A on February 24, 1862. In March he was appointed quartermaster for the battalion. He was promoted to 1st Lieutenant in May and Captain in December 1862. He was wounded on the 31st, but according to his military records he did not die until January 3, 1863. Service Records, Roll 185.

[28]According to the 1860 Arkansas census, John D. Thomas was born in Tennessee about 1837. He and his family lived at Hickory Plains in Prairie County. The census identifies him as a merchant with a real estate value of $400 and a personal estate value of $5,000. In 1860 he was the owner of three slaves. Thomas was elected 2nd Lieutenant of Co. C on February 22, 1862. During the month of May he was promoted to Captain. In June 1862, Thomas and his Negro servant, Joe, became very ill. A local family took them in, but Joe eventually died later that month. Thomas supposedly had a premonition of his death the night before the battle, and he was killed shortly after the regiment captured the Union battery. He and Captain Hammond were buried by some of their men in the nearby McCullough family cemetery. Service Records, Roll 188; W.A. Garner letter, June 18, 1897, Stones River National Battlefield.

[29]James G. Adams was born July 13, 1826, in Sumner County, Tennessee. He moved to

Pruitt[30], and myself were wounded. I staid at this house untill Friday [Jan. 2] and the host was very kind to me. Althou being crowded to excess, he gave me a good feather bed and treated me kindly altogether. That evening Sergts Townsend[31] and Mason[32] and some of the men found me out and brought me the sad news that pour Dave Wright[33] was mortally woundid. One of the

---

Arkansas in 1854. According to the census of 1860 he and his wife, Martha, and three girls resided in Prairie County. Adams, a farmer and slave owner, had a combined asset value of $4,000. The Mexican War veteran enlisted in the Confederate Army at Jacksonport and was elected Captain of Co. I May 8, 1862. Service Records, Roll 185; *Confederate Veteran* 11 (March 1903), 124.

[30]Charles D. Pruet, a resident of Greene County, was born in Roane County, Tennessee in 1827. He married Caroline M. Nelson in January 1847. Pruet was one of four brothers who came to Arkansas in 1857. Two of his brothers later served under his command. According to the 1860 census Pruet was a farmer and owner of five slaves. In March he joined the army at Pocahontas as a 2nd Lieutenant. He was promoted to Captain of Co. D on November 4, 1862. After being wounded in the groin at Murfreesboro, Pruet returned to duty in the early part of 1863 and was later wounded at the battle of Chickamauga. In December he was granted a 60 day furlough from which he did not return. On May 25, 1865, the six foot, light complexioned Pruet was paroled at Wittsburg, Arkansas. He returned to Greene County and became a well respected and successful businessman. Charles Pruet was a prominent Mason and a strong supporter of church and educational institutions. The Pruet family was instrumental in the development of the city of Paragould. In fact, the main street in the city is named after a member of the Pruet family. Captain Pruet died August 20, 1887. Service Records, Roll 187; *Biographical and Historical Memoirs of Northeast Arkansas* (Chicago: Goodspeed Publishing Company, 1889), 167-68; Myrl Rhine Mueller,"Is It Pruet or Pruett?," *Greene County Historical Quarterly*, 4 (Summer 1968), 15-16.

[31]Andrew W. Townsend enlisted as a sergeant at Little Rock on March 15, 1862, at the age of 28. In September 1862 he was elected Brevet 2nd Lieutenant. On December 24, 1863, Townsend was stationed with the Provost Guard. He tendered his resignation on August 5, 1864.   A day later he was sent on detached service with the Pioneer Corps. He was paroled at Meridian, Mississippi in May 1865. Service Records, Roll 188.

[32]The 1860 census shows that Sebastion C. Mason was born in Pennsylvania about 1831. At the time of the census, he was a carpenter living in Little Rock with a real estate value of $1,000. He enlisted in Little Rock in March 1862 as a private. Mason was appointed 4th sergeant June 17, 1862, and was elected 3rd Lieutenant in January 1863. By the end of the year he was a 2nd Lieutenant. Mason was wounded July 4, 1864, in the battle of Atlanta and died there July 27, 1864. Service Records, Roll 187.

[33]David J. Wright, a 23 year old Lieutenant, was also born in Pennsylvania. In the 1860 census, Wright, a painter by trade, was living in the household of John Runnels. In this same household were several other handymen including Sebastion Mason. Wright joined for duty in Little Rock in March 1862 as a 3rd Lieutenant. In June he was promoted to 1st Lieutenant. Service Records, Roll 188.

men, private Boue, staid with me and paid good attention to me.[34] On Friday Dr. Orme took all the wounded of our Regt into town.[35] Hear I met Lieut Wright. Poor boy, he was a terrible sight. A fragment of shell struck him under the chin cutting away everything except the windpipe. He lingered untill the 15th Feb when he died.[36] He suffered much and bore it bravely. He thought he'd recover. I realy think he would if he had proper care. After I got to town I began to think most of my troubles were over. We certainly had the best of the fight. But on Sunday night [Jan. 4] a officer came to the hospital an told all that was able to go to the depot and get on the cars. He came to me and asked if I was badly wounded. I told him how I was. He said Genrl Braggs orders were very strict about leaving officers behind.[37] I then asked

---

[34]Francis Bowie enlisted in Little Rock on March 15, 1862. He was born about 1836. His service record identifies him as being captured December 31, 1862, and paroled January 10, 1863. If O'Brien's recollections are correct, then Bowie was most likely captured sometime after January 2, 1863, instead of December 31st. Service Records, Roll 185.

[35]Lewis Heck Orme was born on January 25, 1836, in Baldwin County, Georgia. After graduating from the University of New York in 1857, he returned to the South. He practiced medicine for a year in Louisiana and Mississippi, but in the spring of 1858, he moved to Camden, Arkansas, becoming a well respected physician. In June 1861, he was appointed Surgeon of the 6th Arkansas Infantry Regiment. In September he re-signed his position and joined Solon Borland's Cavalry Regiment. He served in that unit until March 1862 when he was assigned to Charles J. Turnbull's Battalion. Orme was appointed Regimental Surgeon of the 30th Arkansas in July 1862. The last mention in his service record lists him as being stationed at Pollard, Alabama in August 1864. Service Records, Roll 187; Gammage, *The Camp, The Bivouac, and The Battlefield*, 140-41.

[36]Lieutenant Wright's Service Record identifies two different dates, February 1st and February 5th, as his date of death.

[37]General Braxton Bragg was in command of the Army of Tennessee at this time. He was born March 22, 1817 in Warrenton, North Carolina. A graduate of West Point, Bragg served in the Seminole War and in the Mexican War. He resigned from the army in 1856 and became a planter in Louisiana. In March 1861 he was appointed brigadier general in the southern army. In September he was promoted to major general, and after the death of Albert Sidney Johnston at Shiloh, Bragg was promoted to general in the Confederate Army. In June 1862 he became commander of the Army of Tennessee, replacing P.G.T. Beauregard. In August Bragg launched an unsuccessful invasion of Kentucky. He later led the rebels to victory at Chickamauga, but resigned shortly after his loss at Chatta-nooga in November 1863. At the request of Jefferson Davis, he went to Richmond and was later involved in the Eastern Theater until the end of the war. After the war he became the chief engineer of Alabama. He later moved to Galveston, Texas, were he died in 1876. Warner, *Generals in Gray*, 30-31.

him if we were retreating. He replied in the afirmative.[38] I said I did not want to be left behind. He told me he'd send an ambulance and have me brought to the depot. He went off and that was the last of it. I sent all around town to try and hire a conveyance to carry me off, but to no purpose. So I had to remain. The yankeys came in [the] next day.

For several days all was confusion and our wounded suffered severly for want of the nesasary food and medicine. But the most appaling sight of all was the number of dead boddies that lay in every derection in the large store that we used for a hospital. There they lay for several days and as they became decomposed the stinch was unbearable. Every night more or less wonded die and their peircing cries for help I never can forget. It frequently happened that two wounded men were put in the same bed and we seen one wake up in the morning and find his bedfellow stiff in death. This was no rare occurrence. After some time the enemy found us all out and provided for us and to the credit of the yanky surgeons be it recorded, they paid much more attention to our wounded than our surgeons did. As an instance of this I may record the fact that the peice of shell that struck Dave Wright was actually left in his neck for 15 days and then it was found and cut out by an Irish doctor named Boyle in the yanky service.[39] Many of our poor fellows

---

[38]While the Rebels got the best of the Federals on New Year's Eve, the following days did not go quite as well. Bragg expected to find the Federals gone the next morning, but unfortunately for the Confederates, they were still on the field. Both sides spent the first day of the new year repositioning their forces. On January 2 Bragg decided to launch an attack on a Union position on the east side of the river. He planned the attack for 4:00 p.m. and ordered General Breckinridge's division to make the assault. John C. Breckinridge, a former Vice-President of the United States and proud Kentuckian, pro-tested vehemently. He and other subordinates thought the planned attack against the strong Union position was pure madness. Nevertheless, at the appointed time and in driving freezing rain and sleet, the division that included his cherished "Orphan Bri-gade" stepped off to begin their assault. The attack was initially a success, but massed Union artillery soon decimated their ranks, and in less than an hour Breckinridge lost 1,500 men. As the thinned ranks stumbled back, Breckinridge was beside himself. He raged like a "wounded lion" and with tears in his eyes cried: "My poor Orphans! My Poor Orphans!" This ended the battle of Murfreesboro. The Confederate Army of Ten-nessee would begin their retreat at 11:00 p.m. the following day. *OR*, vol. 20, pt. 1, 668-69, 781-88; Cozzens, *No Better Place to Die*, 183, 196.

[39]O'Brien is referring to Charles E. Boyle, who was the regimental surgeon of the 9th Ohio Infantry. In 1849, Boyle served as the physician of a local prospecting company's expedition to California. When the nation plunged into civil war, the forty year old doctor heeded his country's call, and accepted his appointment on May 28, 1861 at Camp Dennison, Ohio. Boyle was temporarily detached from his unit in order to treat the many wounded soldiers following the battle at Murfreesboro. He resigned his position

has cause to be thankful to him. He was from Ohio. I think amongst the many humbugs in the Confederate service the medical dept is the most stupendous. During this time my wounds were seperating freely and I thought two months at the furthest would make me all right. Allas for human foresight. That lothesome and infectious disease known as hospital gangrene began to show itself amongst the more severely wounded and as no effective means was used to check it, it spread with great rapidity. The moreso that all had to use the same vessels in dressing our wounds. Some casses of this gangrene were terible to look on. In the mean time, Dr. Orme left us and went to the Regt. I regreted this. For whatever faults he might have unkindness was not amongst them. Besides he appeared to be the last link that conected me with home and I soon felt when he went that I realy was a stranger amongst strangers and of course I had no preference. Bad as our fare was before it now grew beautifully worse. The gangrene appeared to be bent on eating the maimed limbs off its poor victims. Our surgeons appeared to be tired of us and kept telling us to go to Nashville, where they said there were fine hospitals and good attention paid to the sick. Tired and disgusted with them I resolved to go to Nashville. So on a cold and raw evening about the later end of Feb I was placed in an old filthy box car and I started.[40] We passed by the battle field and altho two months had nearly passed, their were plain to be seen the indelible marks of the feirce strugle that took place there. Dead horses, broken caisons, large trees shattered as if rent asunder with lightning, the earth ploughed and torn with shot and shell bore testimony of one of the greatest strugles that took place in the west.[41] But the most striking

---

on April 29, 1863 because of illness and returned to his him home in Columbus, Ohio. According to the 1860 census he and his wife, Catherine, were the parents of seven children. Compiled Service Records of Union Soldiers Who Served in Organizations from the State of Ohio, National Archives; Alfred E. Lee, *History of the City of Columbus: Capitol of Ohio*, 2 vols. (New York: Munsell & Co., 1892), II, 33.

[40] According to his service record, O'Brien was forwarded to Nashville on February 16.

[41] The victory came at a crucial time for Abraham Lincoln. In the latter part of 1862, the Union sustained a number of military as well as political setbacks. With war weariness reaching a crescendo in the North the Lincoln administration was becoming increasingly disturbed by the growing influence of the antiwar Democrats, particularly in the Northwest. In fact, for a time there was actually fear of a second rebellion erupting in that part of the country. A few days before the news of Breckinridge's repulse reached northern newspapers, the Republican governor of Indiana, Oliver P. Morton, wired Secretary of War Edwin Stanton stating, "I am advised that it is contemplated when the Legislature meets in this state to pass a joint resolution acknowledging the Southern Confederacy, and urging the states of the Northwest to dissolve all constitutional relations with the

and empressive sight that met the veiw was the emance forrest of head boards to be seen in all directions. The enemy had burried their dead hear, but hundreds of them were buried by our men after the fight on Wednesday.[42] We reached Nashville after dark. I was very cold and wanted to get to the fire. Visions of large cheerful fires, warm suppers, and comfortable quarters flited before me, but alas no such things for me. We were kept at the depot untill the roll was called which took sometime. Then we were placed in rough waggons and hauled to the steam boat landing. Hear we had to wait about an hour and a half before we could get on board. At [length] I was brought on board nearly stiff with cold. We were placed on deck with no fire. Indeed my condition was pitiable the more so that I could not excersise or move, but as I was carried I rested that night as best I could. Next day I learned we were going to Camp Morton.[43] Thinking when I left Murfreesboro I was going to

---

New England states." According to Morton, "the same thing is on foot in Illinois." In addition, Lincoln was also threatened by growing dissatisfaction within his own party. Loud murmurings were beginning to erupt in regards to the progress of the war. Only weeks before the battle, Lincoln managed to fend off an effort by Republican senators to reorganize his cabinet. During this crisis, the President remarked "We are now on the brink of destruction. It appears to me that the Almighty God is against us, and I can hardly see a ray of hope." The victory by Rosecrans on the banks of the Stones River helped to quiet and dispel the President's antagonists. Several months after the battle, Lincoln wrote Rosecrans and told him "I can never forget, whilst I remember anything, that about the end of last year and the beginning of this, you gave us a hard-earned victory, which, had there been defeat instead, the nation could have scarcely lived over. Neither can I forget the check you so opportunely gave to a dangerous sentiment which was spreading in the North." Cozzens, *No Better Place to Die*, 205-6; Allan Nevins, *The War for the Union,* 4 vols. (New York: Charles Scribner's Sons, 1959-71), II, 376-95; Theodore Calvin Pease and James G. Randall, eds., *The Diary of Orville Hickman Browning*, 2 vols. (Springfield, IL: Illinois State Historical Society, 1925), I, 596-601; Roy P. Basler, ed., *The Collected Works of Abraham Lincoln*, 8 vols. (New Brunswick, NJ: Rutgers University Press, 1953), VI, 424-25.

[42]The Battle of Murfreesboro December 31, 1862-January 2, 1863, was certainly one of the great battles of the Civil War. It was also one of the bloodiest. The Union army entered the battle with 43,400 men and suffered 13,249 casualties (31%) while Confederate casualties numbered 10,266 out of 37,712 (27%). The 30th Arkansas joined the fight with less than 300 men and lost 95 before the fighting ended. *OR*, vol. 20, pt. 1, 201, 215, 674.

[43]Before the war, Camp Morton had been the State Fair Grounds in Indianapolis, Indiana. Early in the war it served as barracks for a small number of Indiana troops. After the fall of Forts Henry and Donelson the camp was turned into a prison to accommodate captured Rebels. Sheds that had been used for cattle and horses became barracks for soldiers. Other buildings were poorly built, often with no floor. While conditions were certainly not ideal, at this stage of the war things were not as bad as they were to become.

Camp Morton, Indiana

*Courtesy: Massachusetts Comandery Military Order of the Loyal Legion
and the U.S. Army Military History Institute.*

Nashville I took nothing to dress my wounds and after I got on the boat I felt that it was nesasary to dress them. I learned their were two surgeons of our own on board. I sent to them to pay some attention to me when they said they had not a thing in the way of medicine with them. So I had no alternative, but to take off the cloths I had on, rinse them in cold water and put them on again. I think it took us about five days to get to Camp Morton. On this trip I suffered greatly from cold, the more so from the fact that both legs from the knees down had no covering. When I was wounded this portion of my pants was of course clotted with blood and they tore them off. I thought I could get a pair out of my trunk, but I never seen the trunk since. When I got to Camp Morton I went into [the] hospital. Now wheather it was that before I left Murfreesboro the seeds of gangrene was sowed in my wounds, wheather I caught cold on the trip, or that I moved too soon I know not, but I do know that my leg began to get worse rapidly and all the pain I suffered before was nothing to what I began to suffer now. Night or day I could not sleep. The wound next my knee began to slough so fast that in a week it was large enough to bury a large sised apple in it and it burned me as if a coal of fire had been on it. All the time I had to use morphine freely. At [length] about the tenth of May it showed signs of healing. At [length] I got able to sit up and after a while I began to use crutches. Whilst hear an exchange of officers took place, but I was unable to move. I regreted this very much. One more officer and myself was all that was left. This was Lieut Hays of the 2nd Ky.[44] We were at this date still together Feb 22nd 1863. At [length] about the 28th of May we left Camp Morton for Ft. Deleware thinking of course that we'd be exchanged right off.[45] But again I was doomed to disappointment. The last boat load of officers that has left since left Deleware the day before I

Francis Trevelyan Miller, ed., *Photographic History of the Civil War*, 10 vols. (New York: The Review of Reviews Co., 1912), VII, 64-6.

[44]William J. Hays, a resident of Hickman County, enlisted in Co. A of the 2nd Kentucky Infantry on July 5, 1861. He was captured at Fort Donelson February 16, 1862. Hays then was sent from Camp Douglas to Vicksburg for exchange in September 1862. He was promoted to 2nd Lieutenant December 26, 1862. After being wounded and captured at Murfreesboro, he was sent to Camp Morton. In May 1863, he was transferred to Fort Delaware. Lieutenant Hays spent only a couple of months at Fort Delaware and was subsequently forwarded to Johnson's Island. He remained there until being sent to Point Lookout for exchange on February 20, 1865. Hays later surrendered at Washington, Georgia in May 1865. He took the Oath of Allegiance at Nashville on May 22, and was then identified as standing 5'10" with grey eyes, brown hair, and a fair complexion. Compiled Service Records of Confederate Soldiers Who Served in Organizations from the State of Kentucky, National Archives Microcopy 319, Roll 83.

[45]Fort Delaware was finally completed in 1859, after being under construction for nearly

Entrance to Fort Delaware.
Courtesy: Historical Society of Delaware.

got there and even some that went on her had to come back. I found the trip from the west had irritated my leg very much and I had to go into [the] hospital again. I got allong very well for a while, but the fights on Big Black and Champion Hill, Miss filled Deleware with prisoners, many of them sick and wounded.[46] Then all the convalesents had to leave the hospital and go to the fort. Then for the first time since I was a prisoner did I receive treatment that could justly be called cruel. Of the many little, petty meaneses they resorted to to anoy and insult us, it is useless to speak. Suffice it to say that over one hundred of us was shut up in a room not sufficient to accomodate half that number. This in the heat of summer add to this the revolting fact that some of the inmates of this room had wounds the smell of which was so offensive that it was with difficulty their friends could go near them. I experienced this myself the victim being Lieut James A. Black of Florida who was wounded at Murfreesboro.[47] But the greatest nuisance was the sink [latrine] that was in the room with us. The door was kept shut windows kept down nor would

---

ten years. The former United States Secretary of War, Jefferson Davis, was instrumental in it's completion. Though not originally intended to serve as a prisoner-of-war camp, the Fort received it's first Confederate prisoners in April 1862. At its peak there were nearly 12,600 prisoners interned at Fort Delaware. The prison gained a reputation for its poor living conditions and high mortality rate. A Northern physician who visited the Fort called it, "an inferno of detained rebels." W. Emerson Wilson, *Fort Delaware* (Newark: University of Delaware Press, 1957), 7-17.

[46]The battle at Champion's Hill was the decisive battle of the Vicksburg Campaign. On May 16, 1863, Federal troops under U.S. Grant defeated a Confederate force under the command of General John C. Pemberton in a relatively short, but intense, fight along the slopes of Champion Hill. The Rebels were forced to retreat and were then routed from their position on the Big Black River the following day. At the Big Black, the Confederates lost 1,750, most of which were captured, while the Federals lost only 200 men. The Union Army was now only about ten miles from Vicksburg and the Confederates were forced to withdraw into the city. Many have argued that the battle was the single most important engagement of the Civil War. The resulting victory made the fall of Vicksburg inevitable. It also established Grant's reputation as a hard fighter, which eventually resulted in him assuming command of all Union forces later in the war. Had he not been successful at Champion Hill, Grant probably would not have had the opportunity to lead the Union to victory against Robert E. Lee's Army of Northern Virginia. James M. McPherson, *Battle Cry of Freedom* (New York: Oxford University Press, 1988), 630-31; Edwin Cole Bearss, *The Campaign for Vicksburg*, 3 vols. (Dayton, OH: Morningside House, Inc., 1991), II, 637-39.

[47]James A. Black joined the 4th Florida Infantry as a 2nd Lieutenant on August 29, 1861, at St. Vincents Island, Florida. He was twenty-one years of age when he mustered in with other Floridians to fight for the cause of the Confederacy. Black, who was elected 1st Lieutenant of Co. A in May 1862, received a gunshot wound in each leg at

we be allowed papers of any kind. These were only some of the outrages we were subjected to. I could mention many more but enough of Deleware.[48] At [length] an order came for us all to go to Johnson's Island.[49] This news was hailed with delight by all. For I believe we would be almost willing to try pandemonium itself in exchange for Ft. Deleware. On the [July] 18th we left and arrived at the Island on the 20th passing through Philidelphia, Harrisburg, and Pittsburg. We found the Island a much better place than we left. There was [a] sutlers store well supplied with such things as we wanted besides we had plenty of room to walk about and all the papers of the day were allowed to come in. At first we were much pleased at our good fortune. But still the anxious inquiry on freindly meeting would be, what news did you hear, anything about exchange? There was plenty of room as I said at first, but gradually it began to get crowded until at last we had in round numbers 2566 prisoners on the Island. These were all officers except 70. Every room was crowded to excess. The summer and fall slowly passed off. During the fall several prisoners came from various parts of the Confederacy. As the

---

Murfreesboro. He was captured January 5 and forwarded to Nashville May 13, 1863. From there he went to Fort Delaware via Louisville, Kentucky. Black was transferred to Baltimore in February 1864, and exchanged the following month. After being admitted to General Hospital No. 4 in Richmond, Virginia March 6, Lieutenant Black was classified as "permanently disabled" and furloughed home to Quincy, Florida. He was later paroled at Tallahassee May 10, 1865. Compiled Service Records of Confederate Soldiers Who Served in Organizations from the State of Florida, National Archives Microcopy 251, Roll 53.

[48]Another "outrage" suffered by the imprisoned Confederates was the poor sanitary conditions of the camp. The drinking water at the prison was far from appealing. A captured rebel described it this way: "The standing rain water breeds a dense swarm of animalculae, and when the. . . interior sediment is stirred up. . .the whole contents become a turgid salty, jellified mass of waggle tails, worms, dead leaves, dead fishes and other putrescent abominations. . .The *smell* of it is enough to revolt the stomach. . . to say nothing of making one's throat a channel of such stuff." J.G. de Roulhac Hamilton, ed., *The Papers of Randolph Abbott Shotwell,* 3 vols. (Raleigh: North Carolina Historical Commission, 1929-36), II, 160.

[49]On October 3, 1861, Lieutenant Colonel William Hoffman, acting Commissary-General of Prisoners was given an order to locate a Federal prison on one of the islands in Lake Erie. After assessing a number of possibilities, he decided on Johnson's Island, which is located about three miles out into the bay from Sandusky, Ohio. This location afforded a slightly more moderate climate than other islands out in the open water. The close proximity to the city made resupply easy and also lessened the likelihood of uprising by the inmates. The prison was considered one of most secure and inaccessible in the North. The first prisoners arrived in April 1862. Charles E. Frohman, *Rebels on Lake Erie: The Piracy, the Conspiracy, Prison Life* (Columbus: Ohio Historical Society, 1965), 1-7.

Plan of the Military Prison
Situated on the South side of
Johnsons Island
In the Bay of Sandusky Ohio.

THE PLACE OF CONFINEMENT FOR CONFEDERATE
STATES OFFICERS, CAPTURED BY THE U.S ARMY. 1864

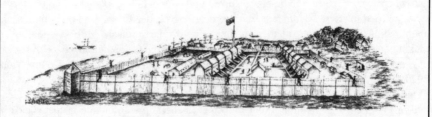

Top: **Map of Johnson's Island Military Prison.**
Bottom: **Sketch of the Military Prison at Johnson's Island.**
Both images courtesy: Ohio Historical Society.

fall merged into winter the weather began to get cold and gloomy. How often did I wish to get off the Island. Sometimes we'd hear an exchange was aggreed uppon. This would keep our spirits up for a fiew days and when we'd think it was all right allas the news would come that it was all grape. Again we'd hear that the commisioners met, but could not aggree. Something about the everlasting nigger busted up the whole thing.[50] Then we'd curse the whole nigger race from Ham down. Of course the D—d yankys would come in for their share. Some would wish every yank in the North was married to a nigger. Whilst we were liberal enough to allow two or three off Harriet B. Stowe,[51] Lucy Stone,[52] and other pious and modest ladies of that class whilst to Mr.

---

[50]The exchange system broke down in 1863, partly over the Confederacy's refusal to treat captured black soldiers as prisoners of war. President Lincoln's Emancipation Proclamation, issued January 1, authorized the recruitment of blacks for service in the Union military. The head of the Confederate Bureau of War summed up the feelings of many Southerners when he asserted, "the enlistment of our slaves is a barbarity. . . no people . . . . could tolerate. . . the use of savages [against them]. . . We cannot on any principle allow that *our property* can acquire adverse rights by virtue of a theft of it." By the end of the year, the Confederates had acquiesced to exchanging free blacks who had enlisted for service, but according to the Confederate exchange commissioner, they would "die in the last ditch" before "giving up the right to send slaves back to slavery as property recaptured." The Union Secretary of War responded by informing them that the captured Rebels now in prison camps in the North could stay there until all prisoners, regardless of color, were treated as equals. One of the consequences of this breakdown was that the prisons soon swelled even further beyond their intended capacity. This would play a role in the development of some of the horrifying conditions of many prisoner of war camps. McPherson, *Battle Cry of Freedom*, 792-93.

[51]Harriet Beecher Stowe's religious upbringing as the daughter of a New England preacher led her to develop a deep disgust for the institution of slavery. This contempt compelled her to pen the wildly popular novel, *Uncle Tom's Cabin*. The book came out in 1852 and was instantly successful, selling over 300,000 copies in the first year. With vivid and moving prose, Stowe depicted slavery as an abomination, leading to unsuccessful efforts to ban the book in the South. Stowe was able to meet President Lincoln in 1862 and he reportedly greeted her by saying, "So you're the little woman who wrote the book that made this great war." McPherson, *Battle Cry of Freedom*, 88-90.

[52]Lucy Stone was the first Massachusetts woman to earn a bachelor's degree. In 1847 she graduated from Oberlin Collegiate Institute in Ohio. It was the only college in the United States that gave degrees to women. Soon after she became a speaker for the American Anti-Slavery Society. Stone was also very active in the women's rights movement, helping to organize the first national convention on the subject. After the war she was instrumental in the organization of the American Women's Suffrage Association. In addition, Stone started publishing *The Woman's Journal* in 1870, which would go on to become the longest running women's suffrage paper in the United States. Elinor

Beecher,[53] Brothers Garrison,[54] Phillips,[55] and other gents of that stripe, we would cheerfully give all full harems of nigger winches if they would consent to keep the question from preventing the exchange of thousands of white men, but no amongst the verry fiew ideas they got nigger is the most prominent and to use a homely phrase they hang on to it like grim death a nigger.

Christmas as last came round and still no exchange was effected. I was now a year a prisoner. I had written several letters home for the enemy was in Little Rock, but as yet I got no letters from there and this troubled me greatly.[56] I also wrote to my Regt, but as yet no letters came to me. John Cunningham who corosponded with me regularly all spring and summer failed to write to

---

Rice Hays, *Morning Star: A Biography of Lucy Stone, 1818-1893* (New York: Harcourt, Brace & World, 1961), 33-34, 74-85, 210-17.

[53]Henry Ward Beecher, the brother of Harriet B. Stowe and a New York clergyman, was an ardent abolitionist in his own right. During the mid-1850's when violence flared in Kansas he shipped crates of Sharps rifles, which were styled "Beecher's Bibles" to the anti-slavery forces in the state. In 1861 Beecher was made editor of the *New York Independent*, which was the largest and most influential political-religious weekly newspaper in the country. He would later resign in the spring of 1863 and travel to England where he initiated a lecture tour to rouse English support for the North. James McPherson, *The Struggle for Equality: Abolitionists and the Negro in the Civil War and Reconstruction* (Princeton, NJ: Princeton University Press, 1964), 88; Paxton Hibben, *Henry Ward Beecher: An American Portrait* (New York: The Press of the Readers Club, 1942), 134.

[54]William Lloyd Garrison was considered a pioneering leader of the militant abolitionist movement. In 1831 he began publishing the anti-slavery newspaper, *The Liberator*. Though his followers were small in number they had a tremendous impact on the abolition crusade. Their radicalism and fiery language sometimes aroused violent public reaction. McPherson, *The Struggle for Equality*, 3-4.

[55]Wendell Phillips was Garrison's most trusted lieutenant. He was also an impressive orator who's words were rallying cries for thousands of people. Phillips, a frequent and harsh critic of Lincoln, was accused of treason by the Northern press after one particularly vicious attack on the President. McPherson, *The Struggle for Equality*, 3, 86, 109-114.

[56]The Federals captured Little Rock on September 10, 1863, after a forty day campaign. During the Federal march on the capital city the Confederate command was plagued by dissension. Generals John S. Marmaduke and L.M. Walker were still seething over a disagreement that occurred during the Battle of Helena two months prior. Their feud reached a boiling point when Walker challenged Marmaduke to a duel after being accused of cowardice. During the early morning hours of September 6, the two met, and Marmaduke mortally wounded Walker, who died the next day. After the capture of the city the Rebels under the command of General Sterling Price retreated to Arkadelphia. The state's Confederate government eventually relocated to Washington in the southwest corner of the state. With the capture of Little Rock, the Federals gained control of

me for several months.[57] All the news I could hear were of defeats to the Confederates. These were magnified to such a degree that the stoutest hearts became despondent. Whilst we well knew the yanky propensty for lieing, still it was quite evident we were losing ground and I suffered much mental agony at this period.[58] At [length] the long looked for letter came from my beloved wife. With what suspense I opened that letter and glanced hurriedly over its contents untill my eye light on the paragraph that told me all was well. My dear little men they were allive and well and growing verry big. My beloved Annie she was well. My fond sister and [her] husband they were also well.[59] This was happiness enough for one day. From the bottom of my heart I thanked the giver of all good that amongst my many trials and sufferings he was pleased to spare those so near and dear to me. I think that I was happier that day than I'd been in two years and that night I dreamed of home of Jaimmy and Johnny that they told me how much they loved me. I thought we all were at Mr. Sinnotts and I told them about my campains and that we had a great time. Generally whilst in the midst of these pleasant visions I heard a great noise. I was startled out of my sleep and they were calling out "fall in for roll call". I opened my eyes. It was all a dream. I was on Johnson's

---

the Arkansas River from the Mississippi to Fort Smith. Thomas A. DeBlack "1863: 'We Must Stand or Fall Alone'" in Mark Christ, ed., *Rugged and Sublime: The Civil War in Arkansas* (Fayetteville: University of Arkansas Press, 1994), 90-94.

[57]I have been unable to identify John Cunningham. There were at least three John Cunninghams in other Arkansas units, but none of them were in O'Brien's outfit, nor were any from Pulaski County.

[58]Indeed, the second half of 1863 was not a particularly jubilant period for the Confederacy. In July Robert E. Lee's bold invasion of the North was effectively checked at Gettysburg, where the Army of Northern Virginia sustained its most decisive defeat of the war. In addition, the Rebel fortress, Vicksburg, was forced into submission after repeated hammering by U.S. Grant. The city had been under siege for a month and a half before the starving Southerners surrendered. Grant would later say, "the fate of the Confederacy was sealed when Vicksburg fell." The last stronghold on the Mississippi River, Port Hudson, surrendered only a few days later. The Confederates won a hard fought battle at Chickamauga in September, but the euphoria of this success was soon tempered by their humiliating defeat at Chattanooga in November. Ulysses S. Grant, *The Personal Memoirs of U.S. Grant*, 2 vols. (New York: Charles Scribner's Sons, 1885), I, 567.

[59]O'Brien's sister, Cecilia, was married to Martin Sinnott in Little Rock on June 12, 1861. The 1860 census identifies Sinnott as a carpenter from Ireland. In 1878 he was elected to the Arkansas State Legislature. Cecilia died very suddenly on June 26, 1879. *Biographical and Historical Memoirs of Central Arkansas* (Chicago: Goodspeed Publishing Company, 1889), 377; *Arkansas Gazette*, 27 June 1879; *Pulaski County, Arkansas Marriage Record Index, 1820-1901* (Conway, AR: Arkansas Research, 2000), 325.

Island, but then I had a letter from home. This at least was no dream and again I thanked God that my family was all well. After a while I got a letter from Mr. Sinnott and ever since I got them regularly. Martin with his usual genarosity has sent me plenty of money and at present I am as happy as a prisoner of war of fourteen months standing can expect to be![60] Besides we've got a new guard or rather an old one. There's a brigade of veterans from the Potomac doing duty hear now.[61] They are much more pollite and courteous than the troops that have been guarding us heretofore and that is inveriably the case for soldiers that have seen service treats their prisoners much more leinintly than home guards. We've experienced that hear. There was a battalion hear known as the Hoffman Bat and I think a meaner set of scoundrels never wore a uniform.[62] If ever they go to the front and our boys get hold of any of them my oppinion is that the great yanky nation will be just that many less in population.[63] I shall never forget Hoffmans Bat!

---

[60]Policy at Johnson's Island allowed prisoners to have money. Often provided by family and friends, these funds were deposited with the post commander and orders from the prison sutler could be drawn against these accounts. With the money, the prisoners could purchase an assortment of items ranging from fresh fruits and vegetables to new clothing, tobacco, writing materials, and other personal items. Prices were fixed by the prison administrators. Occasionally these services were halted in retaliation for privations against Union prisoners of war interred in the South. Frohman, *Rebels on Lake Eries*, 15-21.

[61]A brigade of infantry, under the command of Brigadier General Alexander Shaler, was transferred from the Army of the Potomac to Johnson's Island in November 1863. At that time the federal government was alerted by Canadian officials of a plot by Rebel agents to free the prisoners of the Island. The "Canadian Scare" never materialized, though it did create quite a stir around Sandusky. Rumors of raids occurred throughout the life of the prison. In September 1864, a group of Southern agents seized the steamer *Philo Parsons* in Lake Erie, but for unexplained reasons never followed through with plans to liberate their brethren. *Ibid*, 72-80; E.O. Mitchell, "Johnson's Island: Military Prison for Confederate Soldiers," *Papers Prepared for the Commandery of the State of Ohio, Military Order of the Loyal Legion of the United States* (Cincinnati: The Robert Clarke Company, 1903), V, 119-20.

[62]The Hoffman Battalion was organized in December 1861 specifically for guard duty at Johnson's Island. The original four companies A,B,C,D were transferred to the 128th Ohio Infantry on January 5, 1864. The regiment remained at Johnson's Island for the duration of the war. Fredrick H. Dyer, *A Compendium of the War of the Rebellion*, 3 vols. (New York: Thomas Yoseloff, 1959), III, 1556.

[63]It is interesting to compare the similarity of this statement with a statement made by fellow prisoner, Lieutenant Colonel Joseph Barbiere. He describes one of the officers in the Hoffman Battalion this way: "He has made himself obnoxious, to the entire prison community by his boorish disposition, and his ruffian manners, and will catch many a castigation, if the chances of the field should throw him in the way of some of our gallant

Hoffman Battalion/128th Ohio Volunteer Infantry.
Courtesy: Rutherford B. Hayes Presidential Center, Fremont, Ohio.

Company C of the Hoffman Battalion/128th Ohio Infantry Volunteer Infantry in front of their barracks.

Courtesy: Rutherford B. Hayes Presidential Center, Fremont, Ohio.

At last I've got a letter from Lieut Stillwell.[64] Privates Keely[65] and Baily[66] were wounded at Chickamauga.[67] My Col was also wounded.[68] Allthou this news is not cheering still I am glad to hear from them. They are at Brandon, Miss.

---

men, he has so wantonly insulted." According to Barbiere another of the officers has "little milk of human kindness in his composition" and "takes a delight in irritating those, whom the fortunes of war have thrown under his charge." Joseph Barbiere, *Scraps from the Prison Table at Camp Chase and Johnson's Island* (Doylestown, PA: W.W.H. Davis,1868), 77-78.

[64]Albert C. Stillwell enlisted in Little Rock as a sergeant on March 15, 1862. He was elected 3rd Lieutenant in June 1862 at the age of twenty-one. Stillwell was promoted to 2nd Lieutenant on February 5, 1863, and to 1st Lieutenant in December 1863. He was wounded at Chickamauga. During the summer of 1864, he served on detached service with the Whitworth Sharpshooters. Stillwell was admitted to the Way Hospital at Meridian, Mississippi on February 2, 1865, with a wound and was furloughed home shortly thereafter. The 1860 census identifies him as a clerk working in Little Rock. Lieutenant Stillwell applied for a pension on August 20, 1895. According to his application, he was also wounded in battles at Richmond, Murfreesboro, Atlanta, and Franklin. Service Records, Roll 188; Arkansas Confederate Pension Records, Roll 32.

[65]Thomas J. Keeley joined for duty in Little Rock in March 1862. He was appointed corporal at the time of his enlistment, but was reduced in ranks on June 6, 1862 for disorderly conduct. Promoted to sergeant in the spring of 1863, Keeley was placed on the Roll of Honor for valor at Chickamauga. He was detailed to hospital service in July 1864. Service Records, Roll 186.

[66]Sixteen year old Greenberry Bailey enlisted in Little Rock on March 15, 1862. Born in Mississippi, Bailey worked as a farmhand before the war. He was furloughed home from Selma, Alabama on May 26, 1864. Service Records, Roll 185.

[67]At Chickamauga, the bloodiest battle of the western theater, casualties for O'Brien's regiment were nearly fifty percent. His old company, Co. F, entered the battle with only five men and of those, the three mentioned above were wounded. The losses, which the Southerners could ill afford, were staggering on both sides. The battle while tactically a victory for the Confederates became a strategic loss when they were unable to follow up their triumph and the Federals still held Chattanooga. *OR*, vol. 30, pt. 2, 501-2; Peter Cozzens, *This Terrible Sound: The Battle of Chickamauga* (Urbana: University of Illinois Press, 1992), 534-36; Service Records, Rolls 185-88.

[68]Eli Hufstedler was born January 14, 1830 in Perry County, Tennessee. Following a trip to California during the Gold Rush Days, he returned east, and settled in Franklin County, Arkansas, where he was employed as a school teacher. Hufstedler later moved to Randolph County during the mid-1850's. He married Mary Ann Cude on March 18, 1858. Hufstedler was elected Captain of Co. A on March 18, 1862. He was promoted to Lieutenant Colonel February 27, 1863, and in command of the regiment at Chickamauga. Hufstedler was shot five times while leading a charge on a Union position. He recovered, but was killed in action at Lick Skillet Road near Ezra Church on July 28, 1864. United Confederate Veterans Camp No. 447 at Pocahontas was named in his honor. Service Records, Roll 186; *Confederate Veteran* 9 (August 1901), 359; Lena Jo Kelly

May 1st Several weeks have passed away and still no exchange. Some fiew officers have left for Point Look Out mostly sick and wounded.[69] They have or will be exchanged whilst some others are getting out on special exchange. This system of special exchange I think very unfair and unjust as in most cases they are men who are but a short time in prison. Many of them don't belong to any regular commands. Whilst others of them have been picked up round their homes. The fact that these men can get off whilst other officers who have been in prison sixteen months are overlooked causes great dissattisfaction and they have a just right to complain. But there are rumours of a general exchange. Perhaps it may take place. I for one heartily wish that it may. We have for several days being getting the news of our successes in Ky[70], Ten[71], La[72], and NC.[73] So far the spring camphain is certainly

---

Glaser, *Hufstedler Family and Allied Familes* (Philadelphia: Xerox Reproduction Center, 1974), 454.

[69]The military prison at Point Lookout, Maryland was the largest prison in the North. At times the population neared 20,000. It was located on a peninsula where the Potomac River empties into Chesapeake Bay. Francis Trevelyan Miller, *Photographic History of the Civil War*, VII, 63.

[70]On March 16, 1864, Major General Nathan Bedford Forrest set out with 5,000 men on an expedition into western Tennessee and Kentucky with the goal of harassing the Federals and supplementing his command. Forrest moved against Paducah on the 26th where he "drove the enemy to their boats and fortifications." While there, the Confederates seized a large amount of clothing, several hundred horses, a large lot of medical supplies, and burned one steamer and a drydock, as well as sixty bales of cotton. *OR*, vol. 32, pt. 1, 607-12.

[71]A portion of Forrest's command captured Union City, Tennessee on March 24 and took over 400 prisoners, 200 horses, and several hundred stand of arms. Following his success at Paducah, Forrest returned to western Tennessee where he planned to march on the Federal garrison at Fort Pillow located on the Mississippi River. After his demand for surrender was declined, his men stormed the fort on April 12, and some of them were responsible for murdering captured black soldiers. *OR*, vol. 32, pt. 1, 608-12; Brian Steel Wills, *A Battle from the Start: The Life of Nathan Bedford Forrest* (New York: HarperCollins Publishers, Inc., 1992), 179-196.

[72]At President Lincoln's urging, the Union Army had begun a campaign to secure the cotton and manufacturing center of Shreveport with the additional aim of pushing into eastern Texas. A combined ground and naval force, under the commands of Major General Nathaniel P. Banks and Rear Admiral David D. Porter was to move up the Red River while another land force, under Major General Fredrick Steele, proceeded southward from Little Rock. The campaign met its first major stumbling block at Sabine Crossroads. On April 8, the Rebels struck and then routed the lead elements of Banks' army. Ludwell H. Johnson, *Red River Campaign: Politics and Cotton in the Civil War*, 2nd ed. (Kent, OH: Kent State University Press, 1993), 80-86, 124-41.

[73]A Rebel land force in conjunction with the newly commissioned ironclad ram *Albermarle*

in our favour. Whilst the most unbound confidence is felt in Genrl Lee to [flush] out Grant should he advance into Va.[74] On the whole our prospects at present look quite cheerful. A little while will decide on whose side the fortunes of war will be. For the present we have it all our own way. I seldom hear from home I wish I could get a letter every week. Its now three weeks since I got one. Gold has gone up to 80 cents in N.Y. I wish it may get higher.[75] The prison has been dull for several days, but we look for exciting news every day. There are rumores that Huntsville, Ala will be attacked also that Newbern, N.C. will [be] asalted.[76] Whilst rumour has it that Steele in south Ark will be driven back. Of course I am enterested in any thing that transpires in that direction and look forward anxiously to the result. The weather for several days past has been very cool for this season of the year, but old winter cannot hold sway much longer and we look forward for bright days and a successful camphain in a very short time.

---

assailed the fortifications at Plymouth, North Carolina on April 19 and 20. After a sharp contest, the Federal defenders were forced to surrender the garrison. Included in the surrender were 2,834 soldiers, thirty pieces of artillery, and a large quantity of supplies, all of which cost the Confederates fewer than 300 casualties. Shelby Foote, *The Civil War, A Narrative: Red River to Appomattox* (New York: Random House, 1974), 113-16; *OR*, vol. 33, 305.

[74]In February Grant was promoted to the rank of Lieutenant-General, a position which was last held by George Washington. With this elevation, Grant assumed overall command of all Union forces. He immediately set to work developing a comprehensive strategy that would destroy the Rebel forces and he hoped conclude the war before the end of the year. He envisioned a broad plan where the Union armies in various theaters would go on the move simultaneously and attack Confederate positions. This would be the first ever attempt of a coordinated movement by Federal troops on all fronts. While the other Union armies were doing their part, Grant and General George G. Meade planned to lead the 115,000 strong Army of the Potomac against Lee's 64,000 men of the Army of Northern Virginia. Bruce Catton, *Grant Takes Command* (Boston: Little, Brown, and Company, 1968), 121, 141-70.

[75]The price of gold had an inverse relationship with northern public opinion. The price was a measurement of the value of the dollar compared to the value of gold. The price of the dollar would rise and fall in proportion to the Federal military outlook. The higher the price of gold, the lower the value of the dollar. McPherson, *Battle Cry of Freedom*, 732.

[76]There was no attack on Huntsville, Alabama during this time, but there was a skirmish at Huntsville, Georgia on May 24, 1864. Confederate plans to assault New Bern were foiled after the nonarrival of the Rebel ironclad *Albemarle*. The ironclad, which proved instrumental in the capture of Plymouth, severely damaged several Union gunboats in a three hour engagement on May 5, but was forced to retire after her captain decided she was too unwieldy to proceed on to New Bern. Dyer, *A Compendium of the War of the Rebellion*, II, 665, 707; Foote, *The Civil War*, III, 257-58.

June 8th Since my last entry great events have transpired. As I predicted Steele has been driven back to Little Rock with the loss of his entire waggon team, most of his artilary, and a large number of prisoners have been taken from him.[77] Banks has been driven clear from the Trans-Missippi country with great loss.[78] Whilst the fleet under Porter narrowly escaped capture.[79] So as far as the South west is conserned all has gone well. Sherman has advanced from Chatanooga and several sharp encounters have taken place between his advance and the army under Genrl Joseph E. Johnston but nothing decisive has a yet taken place.[80] Johnston is slowly falling back towards Atlanta. This of course is claimed by the yankeys as a great victory.

---

[77]As Steele headed southward toward Shreveport, his most pressing concern was a lack of adequate supplies. On April 18 the Rebels attacked and captured a Union supply train at Poison Springs. During the course of the battle, a number of Union troops of the 1st Kansas Colored Infantry were executed on the field by enraged Southerners. A week later at Marks Mill, the Confederates seized another supply train and large number of prisoners. As a result of these two devastating defeats, Steele was forced to retreat back toward Little Rock. The Rebels caught the fleeing Federals at Jenkins Ferry on April 30 and in a poorly managed affair allowed them to escape across the swollen Saline River. The expedition was a disaster for Steele who suffered about 2,750 casualties and lost 635 wagons, 2,500 mules, and eight pieces of artillery. Edwin C. Bearss, *Steele's Retreat from Camden and the Battle of Jenkin's Ferry* (Little Rock: Arkansas Civil War Centennial Commission, 1967), 35-37, 76-79, 161-62, 178.

[78]After their defeat at Sabine Crossroads on April 8, the Federals managed to punish the pursuing Rebels at Pleasant Hill the following day, but this success was not enough to convince General Banks to resume the offensive. He ordered a retreat that eventually took them all the way back to their starting point at Alexandria, Louisiana. The repulse endured by the army at Sabine Crossroads combined with the navy's difficulties had undermined Banks' confidence in proceeding on to Shreveport. The loss for Banks' army was approximately 5,200 men, 187 wagons and ambulances, and over 1,000 draft animals. Johnson, *Red River Campaign*, 162-69, 216-21, 277.

[79]Abnormally low water levels in the Red River had stranded the backbone of Porter's Mississippi Squadron, and the ships were in danger of being destroyed by the Rebels. With Porter in a state of despair, Lieutenant Colonel Joseph Bailey of Wisconsin devised an ingenious plan to construct a makeshift dam across the river in order to raise the level of water. Within ten days Bailey and his men accomplished a remarkable feat as the dam stretched across the 758 foot width of the river. A chorus of cheers arose from the bank as the vessels escaped, but the results of the failed expedition were still humbling. The navy lost two transports, two tinclads, and an ironclad, while the army lost an expensive hospital boat and three transports. *Ibid*, 248-50, 260-66, 277-78.

[80]On May 5 Sherman advanced from Chattanooga with the goal of destroying Johnston's army and marching on Atlanta. The first "sharp encounter" took place at Resaca, Georgia on May 14-15, and this was followed by some heavy skirmishing at Cassville on the 19th. After both engagements, Johnston was compelled to fall back. The opposing

Indeed we get news every day of the brillant victories and the wonderful feats accomplished by our (their) gallant army. But the fact is there has been no general engagement their yet and when that comes off my impression is it will turn out like so many other yanky victories the world has heard of for the last three years. The day they will be in Atlanta against the middle of June we shall see. Capt Addams[81] of my Regt has got hear [after] being captured near Resaca, Ga. Page[82] and Edmonson[83] of my Co. were captured with him. The great camphain of the war is open in Va. Over three weeks ago Grant crossed the Rapidan and attacked Lee near a place called the Wilderness.[84] For several days after they comenced fighting we had the usual yanky buncombe glorious vision victory—Terefic slaughter of the rebbels, whole

---

armies met again at New Hope Church on the 25th. Fierce fighting took place on that day and on the 27th at Pickett's Mill. After a failed assault by Johnston on the 28th, the two sides spent the next few weeks struggling to gain an advantage over the other in what Sherman called "a big Indian war." William Tecumseh Sherman, *Memoirs of General W.T. Sherman* (New York: D. Appleton and Company, 1886), II, 30-46; McPherson, *Battle Cry of Freedom*, 748.

[81]Captain James G. Adams was sent to Johnson's Island via Louisville, Kentucky and arrived on May 23. He was released from the Island June 14, 1865, after taking the Oath of Allegiance. Captain Adams stood 5'7" and had hazel eyes, dark hair, and a dark complexion. After the war, Captain Adams returned to Arkansas. In 1897 the United Confederate Veterans Camp No. 1036 at Austin, Arkansas was named in his honor. He died at his home in Cabot January 2, 1903. Service Records, Roll 185; *Confederate Veteran* 19 (February 1911), 80; *Arkansas Methodist* 25 March 1903.

[82]Sergeant James O. Page was sent to the Military Prison at Alton, Illinois. He was paroled for exchange on February 17, 1865 and transferred to Point Lookout, Maryland. Page appears on a hospital register in Richmond, Virginia having been admitted March 4, 1865. This is the last mention of him in his military record. Service Records, Roll 187.

[83]John R. Edmonson was born in Mississippi and before the war worked as an apprentice wagon maker. The seventeen year old enlisted in Little Rock as a private on March 15, 1862. During the spring of 1863, he was promoted to the rank of corporal. After being captured at Resaca he was sent to Louisville and then on to the military prison at Alton, Illinois. On August 23, 1864, Edmonson was transferred to Camp Douglas at Chicago, Illinois, from which he was discharged June 20, 1865. Edmonson died in Faulkner County on February 23, 1900. Service Records, Roll 185; Arkansas Confederate Pension Records, Roll 102.

[84]During the early morning hours of May 4, 1864 the Army of the Potomac crossed the Rapidan River with hopes of delivering the Southerners a decisive blow. Lee, who had anticipated Grant's movement, put his own troops on the move that morning to meet the invaders. The two armies collided about mid-day on the 5th in the tangled mass known locally as the Wilderness. The Federals were initially successful, but the Confederates managed to stem the Union advance, thanks in part to the actions of Brigadier General

devisions of traitors captured, their dead and wounded lying in heaps in front of our lines, Grant in sight of Richmond, Lee retreating in the direction of Danville. These are only a sample of the dispatches recvd from that fountain of truth E.M. Stanton[85] but after all it turns out that Grant was badly beaten at the Wilderness,[86] cut to pieces at Spotsylvania C.H.[87] and after trying in vain to advance had to abandon his position and take up another on the Chickahomoney the same ground that proved so disastrous to McClellan.[88] The Armies are now in front of each other and certainly Grant has suffered much worse than the Confederates. Since the champain opened there is unbounded confidence felt in Lee's ability to end the campain successfully. A fiew weeks more will tell the tale.

John B. Gordon. Gordon, who had been told by his commander, ". . .the fate of the day depends on you, sir!" rallied his men and delivered a strong counterattack. The next day, the two sides resumed their slugging match in the dense underbrush. The Rebels were reinforced by the timely arrival of Lieutenant General James Longstreet's Corps. The fighting went back and forth through much of the day and finally tapered off by nightfall. Douglas Southall Freeman, *Lee's Lieutenants: A Study in Command* (New York: Charles Scribner's Sons, 1944), III, 344-72.

[85]O'Brien is referring to Secretary of War Edwin M. Stanton. A lawyer from Ohio, Stanton had served for a short time as Attorney General in the Buchanan administration. McPherson, *Battle Cry of Freedom*, 324.

[86]The Federals sustained nearly twice as many casualties as the Rebels at the Wilderness, but Grant continued to push south. The greatest tragedy for the Confederates was the accidental wounding of Lee's "old War Horse", General Longstreet. He would be out of the war for five months. *Ibid,* 365-67; Mark M. Boatner, *The Civil War Dictionary*, rev. ed. (New York: David McKay Company, Inc., 1988), 925.

[87]The two armies met again a few days later at Spotsylvania. Lee was determined to stop "those people," as he termed his opponents, from reaching Richmond. This battle bore witness to some of the most horrific fighting of the entire war. Union Colonel Horace Porter described the struggle at a place called the "Bloody Angle": "It was chiefly a savage hand-to-hand fight across the breastworks. Rank after rank was riddled by shot and shell and bayonet thrusts, and finally sank, a mass of torn and mutilated corpses; then fresh troops rushed madly forward to replace the dead; and so the murderous work went on. . . . Skulls were crushed with clubbed muskets and men stabbed to death with swords and bayonets thrust between the logs in the parapet which separated the combatants. Wild cheers, savage yells, and frantic shrieks rose above the sighing of the wind and the pattering of the rain, and formed a demoniacal accompaniment to the booming of the guns. . . ." Federal losses for the entire battle were over 18,000. Undaunted, Grant resumed his methodical movement southward. Horace Porter, *Campaigning with Grant* (New York: The Century Co., 1897), 110-11; *OR*, vol. 36, pt. 1, 149.

[88]Over the course of seven days during the early summer of 1862, Lee aggressively attacked Major General George B. McClellan's army in an effort to drive it away from Richmond. Lee's repeated assailment of McClellan eventually forced the latter to aban-

Yesterday the 7th the Republican Convention met at Baltimore to nominate candidates for president and vice president of the U.S.[89] Abe Lincoln will certainly be nominated. We all look forward to a lively time as soon as the presidential campain opens. I say let them fight. What has pleased me most of any thing is a letter I got from home lately by express which brought me the likeness of my dear wife and children also that of Martin and Celia. This is a great source of pleasure to me. I have got other letters from home lately and I am delighted to know that they are all well. I feared Annie and my poor little men would suffer. Indeed I cannot hide from myself yet the fact that they are in a beleaguered town that may any day become the theathre of hostilities. May God in his mercy save and protect them from all harm and grant that I may soon see them. Martin has proved a friend only for him I don't know what I would do. How anxious I am that this cruel and wicked war may close. Surely blood enough has been shed.

July 4th A fine and pleasant day. Early this morning I was awoke by the discharge of a cannon which called to mind bygone days. The yanks are in high feather, but that confounded and naughty Rebbellion wont go down. Dear me if it only would be so kind as to go down. How pleasant and agreeable it be just to think what a nice time yanks would have setting on plantations of Southren gentlemen, ocupying fine mansions and all for nothing, oh yes, I forget, allways of course in the enterest of God and humnity. Poor little yanks, your bright visions will never be realised.[90]

---

don his Peninsula Campaign. Shelby Foote, *The Civil War, A Narrative: Fort Sumter to Perryville* (New York: Random House, 1958), I, 509-16.

[89]Lincoln was nominated for President while Andrew Johnson, an anti-slavery War Democrat from Tennessee, was nominated for Vice-President. The Republicans now billed themselves as the National Union Party in an effort to attract pro-union Southerners and War Democrats. Lincoln had little trouble securing the nomination since there was no other person of his standing within the Republican Party. Bruce Catton, *The Centennial History of the Civil War: Never Call Retreat* (Garden City, NY: Doubleday & Company Inc., 1965), 374.

[90]O'Brien's inspired defiance may be attributed to the oratory skills of fellow prisoner, Colonel John R. Fellows, who had been given permission to address his comrades on this day. Colonel Fellows "poured forth his thoughts, turning the Fourth of July to the glory of the South even the Yankee guards, who had stopped to listen were spellbound by his eloquence. He had it all his own way and the rebels were shouting like mad. The officer of the day finally awoke to the situation, took a file of soldiers, and brought the speech to a close." Daniel E. Sutherland, ed., *Reminiscences of a Private: William E. Bevens of the First Arkansas Infantry* (Fayetteville: University of Arkansas Press, 1992), 177.

Since my last entry Grant has changed his base again and crossed over to the south side of the James River where his success has been no better.[91] Indeed its been worse if anything. Hills Corps pounced on one of theirs and routed them taking a whole brigade prisoner.[92] He has been beaten or baffaled at every point. He still holds on before Petersburgh but can do nothing. His losses has been terible.[93] In the west Sherman has had no better luck. Johnston plays with and when Sherman least looks for it he pounces on him and punishes him severly.[94] They say they are now within six miles of Marietta. Althou Stanton reported two weeks ago that the Union troops had entered it. One thing certain Sherman has a big job on hand. I don't think he'll ever make much out of Joe Johnston. The summer is wearing away and if they expect to put down the Rebellion this year they have not a moment to spare. Forrest, the brave and gallant Forrest, has again badly defeated them in Miss. He met them at or near a place called Guntown some 35 or 40 miles south of Memphis and ran them clear back to Collierville. With in a fiew miles of that city he took all their artilary and teams and captured some two thousand

---

[91]After their costly repulse at Cold Harbor, the Army of the Potomac crossed the James River on June 14 and moved south towards Petersburg in an effort to lure Lee's army out into an open battle. McPherson, *Battle Cry of Freedom*, 739-40.

[92]While probing Lee's right flank around Petersburg on June 22, two Federal corps inadvertently created a gap between their positions, and into this interval plunged Major General William Mahone's division of A.P. Hill's III Corps. The Confederates quickly snatched up 1,600 bluecoats, who decided it was better to surrender than risk death while trying to get back to their lines. The commanding Union general called the whole thing a "most unfortunate and disgraceful affair." *OR*, vol. 40, pt. 1, 326-30, 366-67, 749-50.

[93]The Federals attacked Petersburg on June 18, but with the disaster of Cold Harbor still fresh in their minds, they performed with markedly less vigor. In fact, some of them flatly refused to obey orders to charge the strong Confederate works. From the time Grant crossed the Rapidan at the beginning of May through the end of this latest battle, the Army of the Potomac lost over 66,000 men. This amounted to more men than General Lee had in his army at the beginning of the campaign. Foote, *The Civil War*, III, 439-41.

[94]On June 27 Sherman was severely punished at a place called Kennesaw Mountain, Georgia. Frustrated by poor road conditions and the repeated withdrawals of his enemy, Sherman decided on a frontal assault of the Rebel position. During the course of fighting, some of the underbrush of the forest caught fire and threatened to burn alive a number of wounded Federals. At this point, Lieutenant Colonel Will Martin of the 1st Arkansas tied a white handkerchief to a ramrod, climbed to the top of the parapet, and shouted "Come and get your wounded; they are burning to death; we won't fire a gun till you get them away. Be quick!" Once the wounded were carried off, the fighting resumed. Where the Union troops moved on the main Confederate battle line, their losses reached a staggering ratio of ten to one. According to one young northern soldier, "the men were mowed down like grass." Albert Castel, *Decision in the West: The Atlanta*

prisoners. Its considered one of the most brilliant feats of the war.[95] In the mean time events have been developing themselves in other directions which look very ominous for the yanky nation. I allude to their finances. Gold has gone up to two fifty and still rising. Indeed they are beginning to see that they are getting very poor in more sences than one. Chase has resigned as Secretary of the Treasury and Fessenden of Main is appointed in his place.[96] Lincoln has been nominated for President and Johnson for Vice President. In the mean time another wing of the party has nominated Fremont and Cochrane.[97] So I think they'll have a lively time between themselves. The

---

Campaign of 1864 (Lawrence: University Press of Kansas, 1992), 285-320.

[95] As Sherman moved into Georgia, he grew concerned over the possible havoc that Forrest could wreak on his line of communications. With this in mind, he ordered General Samuel D. Sturgis to lead a force of 8,300 men out of Memphis and to "attack Forrest wherever he can be found." The two opposing forces met on June 10 at Brice's Crossroads near Guntown, Mississippi (about 115 miles southeast of Memphis). In the engagement, the Southerners, though outnumbered nearly two to one, badly mauled the superior Union force. The Federals lost over 2,200 men, of which about 1,600 were captured. In addition, the Rebels secured sixteen pieces of artillery, 176 wagons, 1,500 stands of small arms, and a vast quantity of ammunition and supplies. Upon learning of the Union defeat, an infuriated Sherman remarked to Stanton that he would send out another force, and they were to ". . . follow Forrest to the death if it costs 10,000 lives and breaks the Treasury. There will never be peace in Tennessee till Forrest is dead." Wills, *A Battle from the Start*, 202-15; *OR*, vol. 39, pt. 1, 221-31, pt. 2, 121.

[96] Salmon P. Chase, the most radical member of Lincoln's cabinet, always had been a thorn in the side of the President. The two had been rivals in the presidential campaign of 1860, and Chase still harbored resentment at losing out to Lincoln, who he thought less qualified than himself. Chase had very strong aspirations for the upcoming presidential election. In late June the two had a difference of opinion on a Treasury Department appointment and Chase tendered his resignation, which was in fact, his fourth during the administration. This time Lincoln accepted it and remarked, ". . . you and I have reached a point of mutual embarrassment in our official relationship which it seems cannot be overcome or longer sustained. . . ." The next day Lincoln nominated William Pitt Fessenden of Maine, chairman of the Senate Finance Committee, for the vacated position. Foote, *The Civil War*, III, 462-63.

[97] Discontent with Lincoln's war policies and a distaste for the platform of the Democrats, led a group of radical Republicans, German-Americans, and War Democrats to hold a convention in Cleveland to nominate a third party candidate for president. The convention opened on May 31, 1864, but failed to draw much of a crowd. It was conspicuous for its lack of prominent Republicans. Former explorer and general John C. Fremont was approved by acclamation, and General John Cochrane of New York was nominated for Vice-President. The platform called for a constitutional amendment to abolish slavery, confiscation of rebel lands, a one-term presidency, support for free speech and a free press, and congressional control over reconstruction. Political considerations eventually led Fremont to withdrawal from the race in late September. He feared his candi-

Democrats hold their convention at Chicago on the 29th Aug. I am eagre to see it come off as I expect to see a lively time of it between them. On the whole I feel satisfied that the affairs of the Confederacy never looked brighter. Indeed when I contrast public affairs with the way [they] looked one year ago, I think the people of the South have much cause to rejoice. I hope and trust the worst is past and that I will get out of hear this fall. I feel very painfully the continued seperation from my wife and children, but I hope I'll soon see them. I set some day between this and next Dec for that happy event.

Aug 4 1864 Since my last entry there has been some changes in the situation. Sherman has advanced to within a fiew miles of Atlanta. Johnston has been releived and Genrl Hood has take command of our forces.[98] There has been severe fighting on the 20[99], 22[100], and 28[101] of July. In those fights Hood was

---

dacy would lead to a split in the Republican vote and result in a Democratic victory, which he considered to be much worse than another four years under Lincoln. Allan Nevins, *Fremont: Pathmarker of the West* (New York: Appleton-Century Company, 1939), 568-81.

[98]Jefferson Davis had become disappointed and frustrated by General Joseph Johnston's strategic withdrawals, so on July 17 he relieved him of his command and replaced him with General John Bell Hood. Hood was a proven fighter, but whether he was qualified to command the army is open to debate. Robert E. Lee actually recommended against his promotion. In addition, Hood's ascension was not very popular with most men in the ranks for they had great fondness for "Old Joe". Castel, *Decision in the West*, 352-65.

[99]On July 20 Hood did what was expected and attacked Sherman. After some delay, the Confederates opened the engagement at Peachtree Creek about 4:00 p.m. The Federals, though initially surprised, were able to drive their attackers back in what was a costly repulse for the Confederates. Hood's plan to destroy a portion of the Union army failed because of poor coordination on the part of the Rebels and fierce determination on the part of the Federals. *Ibid*, 365-83.

[100]Undeterred, Hood resolved to attack the Federals again two days later in what would come to be known as the Battle of Atlanta. He sent one corps on a exhausting all night march to hit the Federal left flank. The weary Rebels arrived at their destination late, but moved forward with the attack. Once again, the Confederates were initially successful, but a strong Union counterattack drove them from their position. Hood claimed the battle as a victory though the casualty figures tell a different tale. Confederate losses are estimated as high as twice that of the Federals. A few days after the battle, Hood chastised his army for not being aggressive enough and told them, "You have but to will it, and God will grant us the victory your commander and your country expect." Hood's penchant for blaming others for his mistakes and his poor attitude towards his army resulted in a great deal of resentment in the officer corps and within the ranks. For soldiers to be successful on the battlefield they must have faith in their commanders, and most men in the Army of Tennessee had little faith in John Bell Hood. *Ibid*, 383-414; *OR*, vol. 38, pt. 5, 909.

[101]Sherman kept up the pressure on the Rebel defenders by moving his forces to the west

successful and Maj Genrl McPherson of the yanky army was killed.[102] Sherman is brought up a standing and if he advances again he'll have some hard fighting to do. In Va Grant has disapointed all [with] the high losses of the yankeys. His last great strategy which was to electrify the world has turned out a stupendous failure. True he mined under one of our forts and blew it up, but in the attempt to carry our works after the explosion he was badly repulsed. The negroes were wiped clean out. Their losses are stated at over 12,000. This occurred July 31st.[103]

---

in an effort to flank the Confederates again and cut off the last remaining rail line into Atlanta. Once Hood got wind of this, he sent one of his corps to cut off the Federal probe around his left. The two sides met on July 28 near Ezra Church. What ensued was a furious engagement that saw repeated Confederate frontal assaults fail. Rebel losses were nearly five times that of the Union. "Say, Johnny," one of the Federal soldiers called across the lines that night. "How many of you are there left?" "Oh, about enough for another killing," one of the Rebels replied. Hood's aggressive nature had cost the Southerners dearly in the previous three engagements. They suffered 13,000 casualties during this time compared to 8,000 for Federals. Greatly outnumbered already, the Rebels could not withstand such losses. In describing Hood one noted historian said, "Almost to the point of being psychotic, he associated valor with casualty figures. Success or failure was to be determined by one standard—whether sufficient blood had been shed." Castel, *Decision in the West*, 414-34; Foote, *The Civil War*, III, 486-91; Thomas L. Connelly, *Autumn of Glory: The Army of Tennessee, 1862-1865* (Baton Rouge: Louisiana State University Press, 1971), 430-31.

[102]McPherson was killed July 22 when he unknowingly rode into Confederate lines while trying to restore his own. He was called on to surrender by a squad of Rebels, but chose to flee and was shot through the chest while making his escape. Sherman, *Memoirs of W.T. Sherman*, II, 76-77, 510-14.

[103]Repeated efforts by Grant to seize Petersburg had failed, and the fighting degenerated into a siege. The system of trench warfare that developed here foreshadowed the experience of soldiers on the European continent fifty years later. In an effort to breach this stalemate, Grant reluctantly agreed to a plan submitted by Major General Ambrose Burnside to tunnel under the Rebel fortifications, explode a mine, and launch an attack through that point. The work began on June 25 and within a month the tunnel extended to beneath the Confederate position over 500 feet away. The mine was sprung in the early morning hours of July 30. According to one Federal officer, "It was a magnificent spectacle, and as the mass of earth went up into the air, carrying with it men, guns, carriages, and timbers, and spread out like an immense cloud. . . ." The explosion scattered the Rebels and also the Union troops lined up for the attack. The resulting crater was about 30 feet deep, 60 feet wide, and 170 feet long. The Federals reformed their lines and pushed forward. Instead of attacking around the crater as directed, many soldiers ventured into it. The Southerners recovered from their shock and the result was like shooting fish in a barrel. Into this fiasco plunged the colored division of the IX Corps. They had hoped to prove their meddle, and according to one commander, they exhibited "fighting qualities that I never saw surpassed in the war." However, their

Meanwhile the Confederates are carrying through Pennsylvania and Maryland and threatening Washington itself.[104] Chambersburg has been burned and Crook and other comanders of the enemy have been badly beaten by Early, McCausland, and other brave and daring spirits of the South.[105] On the whole the cause of the South never looked brighter. The peace party in the north is gaining strength every day and every thing looks well for a peace candidate for President.[106] I hope they may succeed.

---

position was too weak, and the Confederate counterattack too strong, and the Federals fled in disorder. Union casualties were not 12,000. They numbered around 4,000, of which a large number were captured. The costly defeat led to an investigation and General Grant pronounced it "the saddest affair I have witnessed in the war." *OR*, vol. 40, pt. 1, 17, 163-67, 787-93; William H. Powell, "The Battle of the Petersburg Crater," Robert Underwood Johnson and Clarence Clough Buel, eds., *Battles and Leaders of the Civil War*, 4 vols. (New York: Century Company, 1887), IV, 545-60; Henry Goddard Thomas, "The Colored Troops at Petersburg," *Battles and Leaders of the Civil War*, IV, 563-67.

[104]In June Lee detached a corps of his army and placed it under the command of Lieutenant General Jubal Early and sent them down the Shenandoah Valley to act as a diversionary force. He hoped to relieve pressure on his beleaguered army and force Grant to detach a portion of his army to deal with this new threat. Early also had orders to march onto Washington, if feasible. Early's army crossed the Potomac River on July 4 and moved to the very outskirts of the capital. The city had strong defenses, but these were severely undermanned because Grant had called most of the garrison away to serve as replacements for the casualties he suffered in Virginia during the current campaign. Frantic pleas from the federal government forced Grant to detach the veteran VI Corps and portion of the XIX Corps. The appearance of these reinforcements prompted Early to end any thoughts of an attack and he ordered a withdrawal on the 12th. During the retreat the general remarked to another officer, "We haven't taken Washington, but we've scared Abe Lincoln like hell!" Charles C. Osborne, *Jubal: The Life and Times of General Jubal A. Early, CSA* (Chapel Hill, NC: Algonquin Books of Chapel Hill, 1992), 245-93; *OR*, vol. 37, pt. 1, 346-49.

[105]On July 24 the Rebels routed an opposing force under the command of Brigadier General George Crook near Kernstown, Virginia. On the 28th Early ordered two cavalry brigades under the command of Brigadier General John McCausland to raid Chambersburg, Pennsylvania in retaliation for one Federal officer's campaign of terror against civilians in Virginia. The Confederate soldiers demanded $500,000 in restitution and if the demand was not met, the town was to be "fired." The townspeople refused to pay, and the city was burned. Osborne, *Jubal*, 250, 302-06.

[106]The summer of 1864 was the darkest period of the war for the North. Grant was being called a "butcher" for his mounting losses in Virginia. This combined with Sherman's apparent inability to take Atlanta led many Northerners to clamor for peace. Many Southerners hoped that if they could only hold out until the election their lot might improve with a Democrat in the White House. Lincoln's unpopular call for 500,000 more troops led the federal government to prepare for more draft riots. The outcry was so strong against Lincoln that for a time he even considered the abandonment of emancipation in

I have just got a letter from home which gives me great pleasure as I've not got one in a long time before. Annie tells me they are all well. This is a great blessing. I have also got a letter from Thos Sheridan.[107] My health is very good and if I could but see my family I think I'd be the hapiest man in Dixie, but alas, that boon is denied me. Well there is an old proverb which says the darkest hour is the hour before day. I hope it may turn out so in my case. At all events I must wish and wait. Perhaps again I make another entry things may look brighter. The Chicago convention will be over and then we'll see what we will see.

Sept 9th Well the Chicago convention has met and adjourned. The result of that is the nomination of Geo. B. McClellen for president and Geo H. Pendleton for vice president.[108] McClellen has declared for the restoration of the union. Wheather he can accomplish it or not is another thing. The war in the mean time rages feircley in the South, and if I except the recent reverses at Mobile Bay[109] and Atlanta[110], the camphain of 64 has been decidely in favour of the South.

---

exchange for peace, but later he thought better of it. On August 23 Lincoln wrote his cabinet, "it seems exceedingly probable that this Administration will not be re-elected." McPherson, *Battle Cry of Freedom*, 742, 758-71; Foote, *The Civil War*, III, 548-49; Basler, *The Collected Works of Abraham Lincoln*, VII, 514.

[107]I have been unable to identify this individual. There is no Thomas Sheridan listed in the Arkansas 1860 census, but there was an Irishman named John Sherden living in Pulaski County at the time.

[108]McClellan, the former commander of the Army of the Potomac and a War Democrat, was somewhat at odds with a portion of the Democratic Party. One wing of the party called for peace at any cost while McClellan would only accept peace with re-union. The Democrats bridged the gap between the two factions by nominating for vice-president, Ohio Congressman Pendleton, who was a staunch supporter of the peace movement. Catton, *Never Call Retreat*, 381-82, 390-91.

[109]The Union Navy steamed into Mobile Bay on August 5 and engaged the massive forts guarding the approach. The Confederates had laid mines, then called torpedoes, in the channel. The lead Union vessel was sunk by one of these torpedoes, and this resulted in the ships becoming bottled up under the guns of the nearby forts. At this juncture, Rear Admiral David Farragut, who had been lashed to the mast of his flagship, yelled his immortal words, "Damn the torpedoes! Full speed ahead." The fleet pushed forward and moved into the bay where it destroyed a Rebel flotilla sent out to face it. The forts guarding the bay were eventually captured in a three week campaign by the Federal navy and army. Thus the Rebels lost the last blockade-running port in the Gulf east of Texas. McPherson, *Battle Cry of Freedom*, 761.

[110]After being repeatedly bested by Sherman, Hood was forced to evacuate Atlanta on September 1. Sherman's army marched into the city the next day. The news of this

The affair at Reams Station on the Weldon R.R. Va has been a great success.[111] Althou the yankeys as usual claim a great victory. Genrl Earley still holds the valley, but according to yanky despatches carefully noted he has been driven within the last month a distance of exactly 30.000.000 miles, but the truth is his main force is but a very short distance from the Patomoc, whilst his videtts [mounted sentries] picket that stream.[112] Wheeler is approaching in Shermans rear and is wreaking things up round Murfreesboro and all through that section of country. The opinion is that he will interfere seriously with the communications of the yankeys at Atlanta.[113] News from Arks states that gun boats on the White River have been sunk and Devalls is threatened.[114]

---

victory and Mobile Bay electrified the North. Secretary of State Seward remarked, "Sherman and Farragut have knocked the bottom out of the Chicago platform." A sullen gloom pervaded the Southern landscape. One dejected diarist summed up the feeling of despair for many Southerners when she wrote, "We are going to be wiped off the earth." *Ibid*, 774-75.

[111]On August 25 the Confederates struck the Union II Corps while it was engaged in the destruction of a section of the Petersburg and Weldon Railroad. In the fight some of the Federal units performed very poorly, largely because they were new and untested. According to the commanding general, one brigade "could neither be made to go forward nor fire." The Rebels captured over 2,000 prisoners, 3,000 stand of arms, nine pieces of artillery, and twelve stand of colors while losing just over 700 men. *OR*, vol. 42, pt. 1, 221-29, 940; Freeman, *Lee's Lieutenants*, III, 589-90.

[112]It is true that the Rebels were still close to the Potomac. During the month of August, Early and his new antagonist, Major General Phillip Sheridan, commander of the recently created Army of the Shenandoah, played an extended game of cat and mouse as the two sides sought to out maneuver each other in the lower Valley. Movement by one side resulted in a reactive move by the other. In the course of this movement, the Federals began work on Grant's order to "leave the Valley a barren waste. . . so that crows flying over it for the balance of the season will have to carry their provender with them." Osborne, *Jubal*, 316-27; *OR*, vol. 40, pt. 3, 223; vol. 43, pt. 2, 202.

[113]In early August, Hood ordered Major General Joseph Wheeler to move northward with his cavalry corps and strike at Sherman's lines of communication. Wheeler was expected to prey upon the rail lines between Marietta and Chattanooga; then cross the Tennessee River and disrupt the line from Nashville to Atlanta. The Confederates had high hopes for Wheeler's operation, but he failed miserably. He attacked a few insignificant outposts and managed to destroy only a small amount of track while wearing out his men and mounts. Wheeler's ineptitude resulted in the destruction of Hood's cavalry. During the campaign Wheeler also lost one of his finest brigade commanders, General John Kelly. *OR*, vol. 38, pt. 3, 957-61; Connelly, *Autumn of Glory*, 434-35.

[114]O'Brien is most likely referring to the attack and capture of the Union gunboat, *Queen City* at Clarendon on the White River in late June. Under the cover of darkness, cavalry and artillery from Brigadier General Jo Shelby's command positioned themselves on the

I do wish the yankeys would have to leave Little Rock. I have not had a letter in two or three weeks. So matters stand at present. The everlasting exchange question seems as far from been seteled as ever. Oh how I do wish that they may aggree. I am fairly tired and weary of this prison life. I am now entering on my twenty-first month. It is a very long time. God grant it may soon end. Perhaps against the first of Oct things may look brighter. There is nothing like "Hope".

Oct 6th Another month has passed and still no exchange. A squad of 50 sick left to day. They continue to send off small squads of sick and wounded. Except those there is no exchange. I fear now I'll have to stay hear all winter. There has been some heavy fighting since last month. Sheridan has attacked Early with a large force and compelled him to retreat up the valley but lost heavily in so doing.[115] At present Early holds him in check, and the oppinion is that before Sheridan gets through with his job that he will have to pay very dear for his whistle[?]. The yankeys under Grant has again tried their [hand] near Petersburg and lost it is said some 5000 men mostly prisoners and gained a fiew unimportant rifle pits.[116] So matters go in Va.

---

bank alongside the boat and opened fire at daybreak. The first rounds disabled the engine and a portion of the crew surrendered while the rest made their escape by swimming across the river. The Rebels took one cannon and an assortment of small arms off the boat before approaching Federal gunboats forced them to set their prize on fire. The Federal outpost at De Vall's Bluff was almost constantly threatened throughout the summer as Shelby's men harassed river travel and communication along the White. In August the Rebels struck the railroad near De Vall's Bluff and tore up ten miles of track, captured 450 Federals, and destroyed five small forts. *Official Records of the Union and Confederate Navies in the War of the* Rebellion, 27 vols. (Washington: Government Printing Office, 1894-1917), ser. I, vol. 26, 415-19; *OR*, vol. 41, pt. 1, 280-88, 649-52.
[115]Following Grant's order to "follow him to the death" Sheridan attacked Early at Winchester, Virginia on September 19. There, 40,000 Union troops descended upon 12,500 Rebels, and the two sides engaged in a bruising slugfest. By the time it ended, the Federals had nearly 4,700 men killed or wounded compared to only 1,700 for the Confederates, but the Federals also captured around 2,000 Southerners. The Rebels retreated, and the two armies met again a few days later at Fisher Hill, where the Confederates were routed from their seemingly impregnable position. Early's troops were sent reeling sixty miles southward. *OR*, vol. 37, pt. 1, 25-28, 112-18, 554-57, pt. 2, 558; Jeffry Wert, *From Winchester to Cedar Creek: The Shenandoah Campaign of 1864* (Mechanicsburg, PA: Stackpole Books, 1997), 45, 103, 109-34.
[116]On September 29 and 30 Grant launched a two-pronged attack along the Rebel lines around Petersburg. The Federals struck north of the James River at Forts Harrison and Gilmer. They were able to seize Fort Harrison, which was on the outer line of the Richmond defenses, but were unsuccessful in their attack on Fort Gilmer. Union forces also

In Ten the gallant Forrest has again struck with his usual briliancy. He has captured Athens with 1300 prisoners and a large train together with comisary and quartermaster stores.[117] He is now at work on the R.R. in Shermans rear and rendering valuable services. In the Trans Mississippi, Price has moved from his position south of Little Rock and is gone in to Mo. At last acts he captured Pilot Knob and several other places and is still moving into the heart of the State. He is having the most unbounded successes.[118] I hope and pray that this year will end this terrible war. Surely blood enough has been shed, [but] the uncompromising spirit of this Abbolition party will listen to nothing, and I don't see any hopes of peace unless the Democrats elect their candidate, and I begin to fear that they will not be able to do it. Again my next entry the election will be over. May God grant peace to the country should be the prayer of every good man. I shall look anxiously for the result of the election.

---

struck south of the James River near Poplar Spring Church. There the Federals captured a redoubt and a line of rifle pits, but lost heavily in doing so. In the attacks Grant lost over 6,200 men, of which approximately 2,400 were captured. *OR*, vol. 42, pt. 1, 31, 137, 143; Freeman, *Lee's Lieutenants*, III, 590-92.

[117]Forrest and his troopers had been ordered to prey upon Sherman's supply lines that ran through northern Alabama and Middle Tennessee. On the evening of September 23, the Confederates arrived just outside of Athens, Alabama, which was located on the vital Nashville and Decatur Railroad. The Southerners quickly surrounded the garrison and then waited for morning. The next day Forrest sent a flag of truce to request the surrender of the post. The Union commander declined, but Forrest was able to persuade his opponent to exit the fort and examine the Rebel forces opposing him. In a bit of shrewd genius Forrest shuffled his forces back and forth, thus giving the impression of a much larger army. Convinced that he was vastly outnumbered, the Union commander ordered the surrender of his troops. The Confederates were also able to fend off a relief column that had been sent to the aid of the Federal troops at Athens. Wills, *A Battle From the Start*, 249-54.

[118]On September 19, Major General Sterling Price crossed into Missouri with the hope of bringing his home state into the Confederate fold. Price's army consisted of 12,000 men of which one third were unarmed. He had been led to believe that if a Confederate force marched into the state there would be a popular uprising and he would gain thousands of new recruits. The Rebel objective was St. Louis, but these plans were soon foiled by the arrival of Federal reinforcements there, and Price decided to strike at Pilot Knob. On the 26th the Confederates attacked the garrison there and were strongly repulsed though they outnumbered the defenders nearly seven-to-one. Early the next morning the Federals slipped out of the fort and escaped. Price then began a march toward Jefferson City, tearing up the railroad as he went. *OR*, vol. 41, pt. 1, 625-30; Albert Castel, *General Sterling Price and the Civil War in the West* (Baton Rouge: Louisiana State University Press, 1968), 196-221.

Nov 24th Well the election is over and as I thought the Abbolition party elected their man. McClellan is badly beat on the electoral vote carrying only the states of N.J. Del and Ky. But the popular vote is very close. So much for the election.[119] There has been some severe fighting in Va between Sheridan and Early in which the yankys as usual claim great victories.[120] It appears to me that if they won all the victories they say there would not be a Confederate soldier in the field for the last year. But the fact is the Confederate Army is in better condition now than it has been for the last three years.[121] I wonder if these yanks ever will stop lying. Since my last entry Genrl Price has been in all through Mo and brought out several thousand recruits and large amounts of stores. Genrls Marmaduke and Cabble were captured and are now hear.[122]

------

[119]Lincoln tallied 212 electoral votes compared to McClellan's 21. In popular voting, the margin was 2,203,831 (55%) to 1,797,019 (45%). Overwhelming support from soldiers greatly aided Lincoln in victory. It is quite interesting to note that in effect the soldiers were voting to continue the fighting and not settle for peace. This was certainly a milestone for American democracy. Foote, *The Civil War*, III, 624-26.

[120]Undeterred by successive defeats, Early decided to launch a bold strike at the Federal position at Cedar Creek on October 19, 1864. In the surprise attack the Rebels routed two-thirds of the Union infantry and severely bloodied the other third. After driving the Federals from the field, the hungry Southerners plundered the abandoned Union camps. Unbeknownst to and unfortunately for them the trounced Federals where being regrouped by their magnetic leader Philip H. Sheridan. Sheridan had been away from the camp, and the sound of battle sent him racing for his army. The presence of their commander inspired the Federal troops to rally, and they launched a strong counterattack against their enemy. In the ensuing battle, the Rebels were thrashed by the blue tide and sent fleeing in precipitous retreat. Sheridan managed to turn a humiliating defeat into a stunning victory. During this campaign, the Confederates endured more than just military losses in the Shenandoah Valley. From the last week of September through the first week of October, the Federals engaged in the systematic destruction of the upper Valley. According to one northern officer, "Clouds of smoke marked the passage of the Federal army." On October 7, Sheridan wired Grant that "when this is completed the Valley, from Winchester up to Staunton, nearly ninety-two miles, will have but little in it for man or beast." The destruction of property was estimated in the millions of dollars. Wert, *From Winchester to Cedar Creek*, 157-59, 239-50; *OR*, vol. 43, pt. 1, 30-31.

[121]O'Brien is obviously far removed from the realities of the situation. Perhaps this statement is his attempt to put a more positive spin on what otherwise must have been depressing state of affairs for himself. By this point of the war the Confederacy was teetering on the brink of destruction. Though the Rebel armies still had quite a bit of fight left in them, they did not have the numbers to seriously challenge, let alone reverse, the inevitable outcome they were facing.

[122]After abandoning plans to seize Jefferson City, Price turned westward with hopes of securing more recruits before eventually retreating southward by way of Kansas. Along the way he was pursued and harassed by a growing Federal force sent to expel him from

Sherman is gone no one knows where. There is great things expected from him. Some think he is going to Savanah others that he is going to Mobile others again that he intends to make a turn into Va and get in rear of Richmond.[123] At present all is my story. Against next month all will be known. Forrest has called at Johnsonville, Ten and burned things up generaly burning steamboats and stores.[124] I hear from home regularly. My dear Annie and the children are well. The winter is on us and no prospect of exchange confirmed. [illegible] I'll close for this time.

Dec 20th The news from Nashville is very bad. It appears from the dispatches that Thomas attacked Hood and drove him several miles with great loss. He

---

the state. The opposing sides met in battle just outside of Kansas City at Westport. In the engagement the Confederate army was crushed by the superior Union forces in what was the largest battle west of the Mississippi River. The Federals caught up with the fleeing Rebels two days later at Mine Creek and sent them retreating in "utter and indescribable confusion." It was here that Major General John S. Marmaduke and Brigadier General William L. Cabell were captured. Marmaduke and Cabell arrived at Johnson's Island on November 5, 1864. *OR*, vol. 41, pt. 1, 625-40; Castel, *General Sterling Price and the Civil War in the West*, 222-41; Compiled Service Records of Confederate General and Staff Officers and Nonregimental Enlisted Men, National Archives Microcopy 331, Roll 44 and 163.

[123]On November 15 Sherman's army left Atlanta and began their "march to the sea." Their destination was Savannah and along the way Sherman hoped to "make Georgia howl." Many northern soldiers took great glee in his order to "forage liberally on the country." This system of total war would leave many Southerners embittered for generations. *OR*, vol. 39, pt. 3, 202, 595, 660, 713.

[124]In mid-October Forrest and his command left Corinth, Mississippi for another raid on Sherman's supply line. Their destination was the Federal supply depot at Johnsonville situated on the Tennessee River in western Tennessee. Along the way the Rebels captured a Federal gunboat, the *Undine*, and a steamer, the *Venus*. With these two vessels, Forrest created for himself an impromptu navy. While he distracted the Federals with his "navy," Forrest moved the rest of his troops into position outside of Johnsonville. At 3:00 p.m. on November 4, his gunners opened fire on the unsuspecting garrison. Within forty minutes every boat was on fire. The attackers then turned their attention to the acres of supplies located on dry land. By nightfall the destruction was complete. Forrest's expedition resulted in the capture and destruction of four gun boats, fourteen transports, twenty barges, twenty-six pieces of artillery, and an estimated $6,700,000 worth of property damage. The Rebels also secured about 9,000 pairs of shoes and 1,000 blankets. All this was accomplished with a loss of only two killed and nine wounded. Sherman reported to Grant, "that devil Forrest was down about Johnsonville and was making havoc. . . ." *OR*, vol. 39, pt. 1, 870-71, pt. 3, 659; William R. Booksher and David K. Snider, *Glory at a Gallop: Tales of Confederate Cavalry* (Washington: Brassey's, 1993), 225-35.

claims to have taken 6000 prisoners. The news from Sherman also looks bad for the cause of the South. He is reported on board of the fleet having made a succeful trip through Ga. If the news as reported be true it is the worst the South has met with as yet. But the worst of all is that Genrl Cleburn is killed.[125] Things in genrl look bad.

---

[125]As Sherman marched to the coast, General Hood planned to strike at his supply lines and invade Tennessee while hoping that Sherman would be lured away from the heartland of Georgia. After a missed opportunity at Spring Hill, Tennessee, an angry Hood ordered a suicidal frontal assault upon the strong Union entrenchments at Franklin. The attack commenced during the late afternoon on November 30, 1864, and by the time it was over, the Army of Tennessee would be all but destroyed. Hood decided upon the assault over the strenuous objections of a number of his subordinate commanders. Before the attack commenced one of Cleburne's brigadier generals, Daniel C. Govan, remarked to Cleburne, "Well, general, there will not be many of us that will get back to Arkansas." To which Cleburne replied, "Well, Govan, if we are to die, let us die like men." In one of the grandest spectacles of the war over 20,000 Southerners stepped off and began the attack across two miles of open field. Cleburne's hard hitting veterans were in the forefront of the assault. The charging Rebels managed to breach the first line of defenses, but were soon thrown back by a brutal counterattack which saw fierce hand-to-hand fighting as the two thrusting sides collided. Cleburne was struck down in the front ranks while leading his men on foot after having had two horses shot out from under him. The two sides essentially wore each other out, and after nightfall, the Federals slipped out of Franklin and headed toward Nashville. The Rebel army was decimated by Hood's ill-fated plan and one Southerner wrote after the battle, "The wails and cries of widows and orphans made at Franklin, Tennessee, November 30, 1864 will heat up the fires of the bottomless pit to burn the soul of General J.B. Hood for murdering their husbands and fathers." On December 15, Union General George H. Thomas launched an attack against the remnants of the Army of Tennessee positioned outside of Nashville. The Federals managed to drive off the outnumbered Confederates and in doing so captured 8,500 prisoners. With the loss, Rebel fortunes in western theater were sealed in defeat. Wiley Sword, *Embrace an Angry Wind: The Confederacy's Last Hurrah: Spring Hill, Franklin, and Nashville* (New York: HarperCollins Publishers, 1992), 178-82, 248-55, 266-71, 374-402.

Epilogue

Captain O'Brien remained in captivity at Johnson's Island for three more months before being paroled on March 14, 1865. He was forwarded to Point Lookout, Maryland for exchange and eventually rejoined his command prior to the surrender of Confederate forces. After the war O'Brien returned to Little Rock and engaged in the grocery business. His third son, Edward, was born in May 1870. O'Brien was a member of the Omer R. Weaver United Confederate Veterans Camp at Little Rock. He died at his home April 27, 1913 and is buried at Calvary Cemetery in Little Rock. [BKR]

Confederate Veterans Reunion, Dallas, Texas, 1902.
Captain John O'Brien is in top row, far left.
Courtesy: Old State House Museum, an agency of the Department of Arkansas Heritage.

Appendix A

Company F, 30th Arkansas Infantry, C.S.A. Roster

Bailey, Charles M., corporal

Bailey, Greenberry, private, age 16, wounded at Chickamauga September 20, 1863, furloughed from hospital May 26, 1864.

Bass, Azra, private, muster roll dated November 7, 1862—"ordered to report him as a deserter, not heard from since the evacuation of Corinth."

Bauman, James B., corporal

Beatty, Franklin, private, muster roll dated November 7, 1862—"ordered to report him as a deserter, not heard from since the evacuation of Corinth."

Beatty, Thomas, private, age 20, sent to hospital at Jackson, Mississippi from Corinth on May 3, 1862, discharged from hospital in Little Rock July 25, 1862.

Bell, Henry, private, age 35, sent to hospital at Rome, Georgia April 15, 1863, deserted August 9, 1863.

Berkhead, John, private, muster roll dated November 7, 1862—"ordered to report him as a deserter, not heard from since the evacuation of Corinth"

Bigelow, Richard R., private, deserted July 17, 1863, captured near Jackson, Mississippi July 30, 1863, sent to Camp Morton, enlisted in 7th U.S. Cavalry on August 7, 1863.

Black, J.E., private

Blackwell, David, private, detailed to Humphrey's Battery November 18, 1862.

Bowers, Marcus D., private, age 29, MIA at Murfreesboro December 31, 1862.

Bowie, Francis, private, age 24, captured at Murfreesboro December 31, 1862 and paroled January 10, 1863.

Campbell, Hughtod, died in camp near Corinth, Mississippi May 5, 1862.

Clark, James B., sergeant, detailed as a butcher at Chattanooga July 16, 1862, paroled at Meridian, Mississippi May 10, 1865.

Clinton, Joseph F., private, age 27, deserted August 8, 1863.

Cross, John R., private, age 41, on detached service as a blacksmith at Little Rock April 3, 1862.

Derain, Charles, private

Edmonson, John R., corporal, age 18, captured at Resaca, Georgia May 14, 1864, received at Military Prison at Louisville, Kentucky May 22, 1864, arrived at Alton Prison at Alton, Illinois May 25, 1864, transferred to Camp Douglas August 23, 1864, paroled from Camp Douglas June 6, 1865.

Enloe, Joseph S., sergeant, age 29, appointed sergeant January 13, 1863, died of dysentery in hospital at Chattanooga May 25, 1863.

Faught, John C., private, age 43, discharged for disability (chronic inflation of lung a sequelae of measles) at Priceville, Mississippi June 23, 1862, born Morgan County, Alabama, height 5'7", gray eyes, light brown hair, fair complexion.

Faulkner, A.J., private, appears on a report of Rebel deserters who surrendered in the limits of the Department of West Virginia for the month of April 1865, took amnesty oath April 25, 1865, height 5'8", gray eyes, dark hair, fair complexion, occupation—farmer.

Ferguson, Robert R., private, age 34, sent to hospital in Atlanta April 16, 1863, deserted July 16, 1863, captured near Jackson, Mississippi July 17, 1863, received at Camp Morton August 7, 1863.

Franklin, Andrew J., private, age 22, deserted July 16, 1863, captured near Jackson, Mississippi July 17, 1863, received at Camp Morton August 7, 1863, paroled from Camp Morton and sent to Point Lookout for exchange March 15, 1865.

Franklin, James J., Major, appointed Major June 22, 1862, resigned December 26, 1862, wounded and captured at Murfreesboro December 31, 1862, received at Camp Chase, Ohio January 15, 1863, arrived at Fort Delaware April 12, 1863, forwarded to City Point, Virginia for exchange April 28, 1863, height 5'8", gray eyes, black hair, fair complexion, place of residence—Little Rock.

Galloway, Richard L., corporal, age 45, appointed corporal January 13, 1863, detached as courier August 27, 1863.

Gillam, Robert, private, age 30, left sick at Chattanooga July 16, 1862.

Gordon, Robert J., private, age 29, deserted December 3, 1862 at Manchester, Tennessee.

Harroll, William P., private, died in camp near Corinth, Mississippi May 20, 1862.

Hays, Jonathan, private, "ordered to report him as a deserter, not heard from since evacuation of Corinth, examined at General Hospital in Little Rock and recommended for discharge July 1, 1862.

Hines, Henry, private

Illg, Englehart, private, exchanged for W.B. Washburn November 13, 1862.

Keefee, Daniel, private, age 27, deserted July 16, 1863, captured near Jackson, Mississippi July 17, 1863, received at Camp Morton August 7, 1863, paroled from Camp Morton March 20, 1865, place of residence—Little Rock.

Keeley, Thomas J., sergeant, age 20, reduced in ranks for disorderly conduct June 6, 1862, promoted to sergeant April/May 1863, wounded at Chickamauga September 19, 1863, placed on Roll of Honor for valor at Chickamauga, detailed in hospital July 27, 1864.

Kifer, James, private

Landrum, John F.D., private, absent without leave June 15, 1862, muster roll dated January 14, 1863 in hospital at Nashville, muster roll March/April 1863 "present", left sick in Atlanta May 12, 1863, died in Atlanta June 5, 1863.

Martin, Charles H., private

Mason, Sebastian C., 2nd Lieutenant, age 31, appointed 4th sergeant June 17, 1862, elected 3rd Lieutenant January 26, 1863, promoted to 2nd Lieutenant February 5, 1863, wounded at Atlanta July 4, 1864, died in Atlanta July 27, 1864.

McStay, John, corporal, age 27, left sick at London, Kentucky August 24, 1862, captured and paroled at London September 8, 1862, exchanged at Cumberland Gap, Tennessee September 16, 1862.

Mocklar, Peter, private, age 26, detailed to go to Arkansas November 17, 1862, absent without leave since January 17, 1863, reduced to the ranks from 1st sergeant February 28, 1863 for being absent without leave.

Morgan, John T., private, age 26, sent to hospital from Corinth May 28, 1862.

O'Brien, John, Captain, age 35, promoted to Captain by seniority June 22, 1862, wounded at Murfreesboro December 31, 1862, captured January 5, 1863, forwarded to Nashville February 16, 1863, sent to Camp Morton later that month, forwarded to Fort Delaware May 25, 1863, arrived at Johnson's Island July 20, 1863, paroled March 14, 1865 and sent to Point Lookout.

O'Connell Daniel L., captain, elected 1st Lieutenant March 15, 1862, promoted to Captain June 22, 1862, resigned June 22, 1862.

Otto, Frederick, private, age 28, on detached service at Little Rock since April 3, 1862 as blacksmith.

Owen, John R., private, age 24, left sick at Overton Hospital in Memphis April 27, 1862, given disability discharge from hospital in Little Rock December 17, 1862.

Page, James O., 1ˢᵗ sergeant, age 28, appointed corporal December 7, 1862, May/June 1863 muster roll listed as sergeant, July/August 1864 muster roll listed as 1ˢᵗ sergeant, captured at Resaca May 14, 1864, received at Military Prison at Alton, Illinois May 25, 1864, paroled for exchange at Alton February 17, 1865 and sent to Point Lookout, admitted to General Hospital No. 9 at Richmond, Virginia March 4, 1865.

Phillips, William, private, age 45, left sick at Chattanooga July 15, 1862.

Porter, James P., hospital steward, age 31, muster roll dated January 14, 1863 detailed as hospital steward for regiment, at Breckinridge Division Hospital No. 1, Lauderdale Springs, Mississippi August 31, 1863.

Prater, George W., private, age 25, discharged for disability June 23, 1862, height 5'7", hazel eyes, light brown hair, fair complexion, born Bledsoe County, Tennessee, occupation—farmer.

Price, Francis M., private, muster roll dated November 7, 1862 died at hospital in Hernando, Mississippi.

Schenck, Daniel R., private age 23, had right eye shot out at Murfreesboro December 31, 1862, detailed for hospital duty at Quiutard Hospital, Rome, Georgia April 15, 1863.

Smith, Levi J., private, age 19, left sick at Barbourville, Kentucky August 24, 1862, left sick at Meridian, Mississippi February 12, 1863, muster roll July/August 1864 in hospital at Montgomery, Alabama.

Smith, William S., private

Snow, Silas L., private, age 25, sent to hospital at Tupelo, Mississippi June 30, 1862, muster roll September/October 1862 reported dead at Tupelo.

Stewart, Albert, private

Stillwell, Albert C., 1ˢᵗ Lieutenant, age 21, elected 3ʳᵈ Lieutenant June 24, 1862, left near Bridgeport, Kentucky September 5, 1862, promoted to 2ⁿᵈ Lieutenant February 5, 1863, wounded at Chickamauga September 20, 1863, promoted to 1ˢᵗ Lieutenant December 31, 1863, tendered resignation August 5, 1864, on detached service with Whitworth Sharpshooters August 18, 1864, he was admitted to the Way Hospital at Meridian, Mississippi with a wound February 2, 1865 and then furloughed home.

Stillwell, Asher, private, age 16, discharged for disability June 12, 1862, height 5'7", blue eyes, light colored hair, and fair complexion.

Strohwig, Ferdinand, private, age 27, on detached service at Maryville, Tennessee making clothing, deserted July 16, 1863, captured at Jackson, Mississippi July 17, 1863, received at Camp Morton August 7, 1863, took Oath of Allegiance at Camp Morton May 16, 1865, height 5'6", gray eyes, light colored hair, and dark complexion.

Sutherland, Isaac, private, sent to hospital at Hernando, Mississippi May 7, 1862, muster roll July/August 1862 died in hospital at Hernando.

Sutton, George W., private, muster roll May/June 1862—"ordered to report him as a deserter, not heard from since the evacuation of Corinth."

Swindle, James A., private, age 33, sent to hospital at Murfreesboro December 31, 1862.

Teddor, George W., private

Thomas, U.M., corporal, age 19, left sick at London, Kentucky August 28, 1862.

Tollett, John H., private, muster roll May/June 1862—"ordered to report him as a deserter, not heard from since the evacuation of Corinth."

Townsend, Andrew W., Brevet 2nd Lieutenant, age 28, elected Brevet 2nd Lieutenant September 4, 1863, tendered resignation August 5, 1864, sent on detached service with Pioneer Corps August 6, 1864, paroled from Meridian, Mississippi May 11, 1865.

Trammell, George W., private, age 25, severely wounded in arm at Murfreesboro December 31, 1862, captured at Murfreesboro January 5, 1863, forwarded from Camp Morton to City Point, Virginia for exchange April 22, 1863, on furlough in Arkansas since April 30, 1863.

Tyrrer, James R., private, age 17, sent to hospital at Hernando, Mississippi from camp near Corinth May 7, 1862, left at Somerset, Kentucky October 20, 1862.

Waldon, James A., private, age 38, muster roll dated January 14, 1863—detailed as blacksmith for regiment, deserted August 7, 1863.

Ward, Benjamin L., private

Washburn, W.B., muster roll dated January 14, 1863—transferred to this Co. from Humphrey's Battery, deserted July 16, 1863, gave self up at Jackson, Mississippi July 17, 1863, enlisted in United States service at Camp Morton March 14, 1865.

Webb, James W., private, deserted, not heard from since March 25, 1862 at Little Rock.

Webster, Samuel G., private

Whitehouse, George, private, age 21, muster roll dated January 14, 1863 in hospital at Loudon, Tennessee, muster roll May/June 1863 "present", deserted July 16, 1863.

Williford, Reuben S., private, age 42, left sick in Little Rock March 16, 1862.

Winchester, Elijah, private, age 26, left sick in Little Rock March 15, 1862.

Winchester, William, private, muster roll dated November 7, 1862—died in hospital in Hernando, Mississippi.

Winters, James C., private, left sick at Fort Pillow April 24, 1862.

Wiseman, Charles H., private, age 27, deserted September 28, 1863.

Wright, David J., 1st Lieutenant, elected 3rd Lieutenant March 15, 1862, promoted to 1st Lieutenant June 22, 1862, wounded at Murfreesboro December 31, 1862, died February 1863.

Wright, John A., private, age 27, reduced to the ranks from sergeant for incapability, captured at Murfreesboro December 31, 1862, mentioned in report regarding Medal of Honor for service at Murfreesboro, paroled at Camp Douglas April 3, 1863 and delivered to City Point, Virginia April 10, 1863, admitted to Small Pox Hospital at Petersburg, Virginia April 11, 1863, deserted September 28, 1863.

Turnbull's 30th Regiment Arkansas Volunteer Infantry Battle Flag.
The battle flag of the 30th Arkansas Infantry was captured at Murfreesboro by members of the 2nd Ohio Volunteer Infantry and Battery H, 5th U.S. Artillery. As the unit advanced on a Federal position, the flag-bearer's hand was shot off and he was compelled to abandon the colors.
Courtesy: Old State House Museum, an agency of the Department of Arkansas Heritage.

Appendix B

Following is a list of clothing items issued to members of O'Brien's company at London, Tennessee, November 15, 1862.

Bailey	cap and blanket
Bell	cap
Bigelow	cap and blanket
Blackwell	cap, pants, drawers, blanket
Bowers	cap and coat
Bowie	cap and pants
Edmonson	cap, shirt, blanket
Enloe	cap and shoes
Ferguson	cap, shirt, drawers, and blanket
Franklin	cap
Galloway	cap
Gordon	cap
Illg	cap, pants, and shoes
Keeffe	cap
Keeley	cap and blanket
Mason	cap
Mockler	cap, pants, blanket, and shoes
Page	cap, coat, and blanket
Schenck	cap
Swindle	cap
Townsend	cap
Trammell	cap and shirt
Wiseman	cap
Wright	cap and shoes

Items drawn at camp near Readyville, Tennessee
[date unknown]

Bailey   1 pair of shoes
Bell   1 pair of shoes
Bigelow   1 pair of shoes
Clinton   1 pair of shoes
Franklin   1 pair of shoes

Items drawn at Manchester, Tennessee
[date unknown]

Bailey   socks
Clinton   socks
Franklin   drawers

Items drawn at Readyville, Tennessee on December 23, 1862

Enloe   1 pair of shoes
Mason   1 pair of shoes
Page   1 pair of shoes
Porter   1 pair of shoes [at London ?]
Schenck   1 pair of shoes
Townsend   1 pair of shoes
Washburn   1 pair of shoes
Wright   1 pair of shoes

Appendix C
Food Rations

During 1862 and 1863 Confederate prisoners at Johnson's Island were allowed to purchase additional food rations from the sutler store that operated within the facility. Following is the "mess out" recorded by Captain O'Brien for himself and Lieutenant William J. Hays in 1863.

August 2	potatoes, butter, and pepper	.60
August 8	potatoes and cheese	.70
August 11	cabbage and pickles	1.20
August 13	potatoes, eggs, and mustard	.90
August 18	cheese and cabbage	.45
August 19	potatoes, butter, and onions	1.50
August 25	cabbage and tomatoes	.75
August 28	potatoes	.30
September 1	butter and tomatoes	.70
September 4	potatoes and tomatoes	.80
September 7	pepper, mackerel, and eggs	.90
September 10	potatoes, butter, and onions	1.20
September 13	cabbage and eggs	.45
September 16	potatoes and cabbage	1.55
September 18	crackers and cheese	.55
September 21	potatoes and butter	.70
September 24	cabbage and tomatoes	1.35
September 29	potatoes and pepper	.60
September 30	cabbage and tomatoes	.50
October 3	potatoes and butter	1.25

October 5	cabbage and eggs	.50
October 8	mackerel and cheese	.70
October 9	potatoes and butter	.95
October 11	cabbage and tomatoes	.80
October 14	potatoes and eggs	.75
October 17	cabbage and butter	.60
October 19	tomatoes and potatoes	.80
October 21	onions and cabbage	.45
October 23	butter, mackerel, and eggs	1.10
October 25	potatoes and tomatoes	1.15
October 28	onions, peppers, and butter	.80
October 29	potatoes and mackerel	.90
October 30	tomatoes	.20
November 3	potatoes and butter	1.30
November 5	cabbage and tomatoes	.90
November 8	potatoes and cabbage	.60
November 11	butter, fish, and pepper	1.15
November 13	potatoes and tomatoes	1.80
November 15	cabbage, fish, and butter	1.45
November 17	onions and tomatoes	.60
November 19	potatoes and cheese	1.20
November 21	tomatoes and butter	1.45
November 23	crackers and cabbage	.95
November 25	potatoes and onions	1.10
November 28	cabbage and cheese	.35
November 30	tomatoes and onions	.70
December 2	potatoes and butter	1.50
December 6	cabbage and tomatoes	.95
December 9	potatoes and butter	1.70
December 11	fish and cabbage	.90
December 13	potatoes and fish	.95

Bibliography

Primary Sources: Manuscripts

Garner, W.A. Letter. Stones River National Battlefield, Murfreesboro, TN.
O'Brien, John. Diary. Old State House Museum, Little Rock, AR.
Widney, Lyman S. Diary. Stones River National Battlefield.

Primary Sources: Newspapers

Arkansas Democrat, Little Rock.
Arkansas Gazette, Little Rock.
Arkansas Methodist, Little Rock.
Northern Indianian, Warsaw.
True Democrat, Little Rock.

Primary Sources: Public Documents

Arkansas Confederate Pension Records, Arkansas History Commission.
U.S. Census Bureau. Population Schedules [Free] of the Eighth United
          States Census, 1860, Arkansas. National Archives Microcopy No.
          653, Rolls 37-52.
_____. Population Schedules [Free] of the Seventh United States Census,
          1850, Arkansas. National Archives Microcopy No.432, Rolls 25-31.
_____. Population Schedules [Slave] of the Eighth United States Census,
          1860, Arkansas. National Archives Microcopy No. 653, Rolls 53-
          54.
_____. Population Schedules of the Eighth United States Census, 1860,

Ohio. National Archives Microcopy No. 653, Roll 964.

U.S. War Department. Compiled Service Records of Confederate General
and Staff Officers and Non-Regimental Enlisted Men. National Archives Microcopy No. 331.

_____. Compiled Service Records of Confederate Soldiers Who Served
in Organizations from the State of Arkansas. National Archives
Microcopy No. 317, Rolls 185-88.

_____. Compiled Service Records of Confederate Soldiers Who Served
in Organizations from the State of Florida. National Archives
Microcopy No. 251, Roll 53.

_____. Compiled Service Records of Confederate Soldiers Who Served
in Organizations from the State of Kentucky. National Archives
Microcopy No. 319, Roll 83.

_____. Compiled Service Records of Union Soldiers Who Served in
Organizations from the State of Ohio. National Archives.

_____. Index to Service Records of Confederate Soldiers Who Served
in Organizations from the State of Arkansas. National Archives
Microcopy No. 376.

_____. Index to Service Records of Confederate Soldiers Who Served
in Organizations from the State of Florida. National Archives
Microcopy No. 225, Roll 1.

_____. Index to Service Records of Confederate Soldiers Who Served
in Organizations from the State of Kentucky. National Archives
Microcopy No. 377, Roll 6.

_____. Index to Service Records of Union Soldiers Who Served in
Organizations from the State of Ohio. National Archives Microcopy
No. 522, Roll 11.

_____. *War of the Rebellion: A Compilation of the Official Records of
the Union and Confederate Armies*. 70 vols. in 128 books and
index. Washington: Government Printing Office, 1880-1901.

_____. *Official Records of the Union and Confederate Navies in the
War of the Rebellion.*27 vols. Washington: Government Printing
Office, 1894-1917.

Primary Sources: Books and Articles

Barbiere, Joseph. *Scraps from the Prison Table at Camp Chase and Johnson's
Island*. Doylestown, PA: W.W.H. Davis, 1868.

Basler, Roy P., ed. *The Collected Works of Abraham Lincoln*. 8 vols. New
Brunswick, NJ: Rutgers University Press, 1953-55.

Bickham, William Denison. *Rosecrans' Campaign with the Fourteenth*

Army Corps or the Army of the Cumberland: A Narrative of Personal Observations with . . .Official Reports of the Battle of Stone River. Cincinnati: Moore, Wilstach, Keys, & Co., 1863.

Biographical and Historical Memoirs of Northeast Arkansas. Chicago: Goodspeed Publishing Company, 1889.

Biographical and Historical Memoirs of Central Arkansas. Chicago: Goodspeed Publishing Company, 1889.

Confederate Veteran. 40 vols. Nashville, Tenn., 1893-1932.

Cowles, Calvin D., compl. *Atlas to Accompany the Official Records of the Union and Confederate Armies.* Washington: Government Printing Office, 1891-95.

Douglas, Lucia Rutherford, ed. *Douglas's Texas Battery, CSA.* Tyler, TX: Smith County Historical Society, 1966.

Fitch, John. *Annals of the Army of the Cumberland: Comprising Biographies, Descriptions of Departments, Accounts of Expeditions, Skirmishes, and Battles; Also Its Police Record of Spies, Smugglers, and Prominent Rebel Emissaries. Together with Anecdotes, Incidents, Poetry, Reminiscences, etc. And Official Reports of the Battle of Stone River and of the Chickamauga Campaign.* Philadelphia: J.B. Lippincott and Co., 1864.

Gammage, Washington, Lafayette. *The Camp, the Bivouac, and the Battlefield; being a History of the Fourth Arkansas Regiment, from Its First Organization down to the Present Date: Its Campaigns and Its Battles, with an Occasional Reference to the Current Events of the Times, including Biographical Sketches of Its Field Officers and Others of the "Old Brigade." The Whole Interspersed Here and There with Descriptions of Scenery, Incidents of Camp Life, Etc.* Selma, AL: Cooper & Kimball, 1864.

Grant, Ulysses S. *The Personal Memoirs of U.S. Grant.* 2 vols. New York: Charles Scribner's Sons, 1885.

Hamilton, J.G. de Roulhac, ed. *The Papers of Randolph Abbott Shotwell.* 3 vols. Raleigh: North Carolina Historical Commission, 1929-36.

Hughes, Nathaniel Cheairs, Jr., ed. *Liddell's Record.* Baton Rouge: Louisiana State University Press, 1997.

Johnson, Robert Underwood and Clarence Clough Buell, eds. *Battles and Leaders of the Civil War.* 4 vols. New York: Century Company, 1887.

Mitchell, E.O. "Johnson's Island: Military Prison for Confederate Soldiers." *Papers Prepared for the Commandery of the State of Ohio, Military Order of the Loyal Legion of the United States.* vol. 5. Cincinnati: The Robert Clarke Company, 1903.

Obreiter, John. *The Seventy-Seventh Pennsylvania at Shiloh: History of the Regiment*. Harrisburg: Harrisburg Publishing Company, 1905.

Pease, Theodore Calvin and James G. Randall, eds. *The Diary of Orville Hickman Browning*. 2 vols. Springfield: Illinois State Historical Society, 1925.

Sherman, William Tecumseh. *Memoirs of General W.T. Sherman*. 2 vols. New York: D. Appleton and Company, 1886.

Sutherland, Daniel E., ed. *Reminiscences of a Private: William E. Bevens of the First Arkansas Infantry*. Fayetteville: University of Arkansas Press, 1992.

Worley, Ted R., ed. *They Never Came Back: The War Memoirs of Captain John W. Lavender, C.S.A.* Pine Bluff: The Southern Press, 1956.

Secondary Sources: Books and Articles

Allen, Desmond Walls, compl. *Index to Arkansas Confederate Soldiers*. 3 vols. Conway, AR: D.W. Allen, 1990.

_____. *Arkansas' Mexican War Soldiers*. Conway, AR: Arkansas Research, 1988.

Bearss, Edwin Cole. *The Campaign for Vicksburg*. 3 vols. Dayton, OH: Morningside House, Inc., 1991.

_____. *Steele's Retreat from Camden and the Battle of Jenkin's Ferry*. Little Rock: Arkansas Civil War Centennial Commission, 1967.

Boatner, Mark M. III. *The Civil War Dictionary*. Revised ed. New York: David McKay Company, 1988.

Bonner, Kathryn Rose, ed. *Arkansas 1860 U.S. Census Index*. Marianna, AR: Kathryn R. Bonner, 1984.

Booksher, William R. and David K. Snider. *Glory at a Gallop: Tales of Confederate Cavalry*. Washington: Brassey's, 1993.

Castel, Albert. *Decision in the West: The Atlanta Campaign of 1864*. Lawrence: University Press of Kansas, 1992.

_____. *General Sterling Price and the Civil War in the West*. Baton Rouge: Louisiana State University Press, 1968.

Catton, Bruce. *Grant Takes Command*. Boston: Little, Brown, and Company, 1968.

_____. *The Centennial History of the Civil War*. 3 vols. Garden City, NY: Doubleday & Company. 1961-65.

Christ, Mark, ed. *Rugged and Sublime: The Civil War in Arkansas*. Fayetteville: University of Arkansas Press, 1994.

Connelly, Thomas. *Autumn of Glory: The Army of Tennessee, 1862-1865*. Baton Rouge: Louisiana State University Press, 1971.

Cozzens, Peter. *No Better Place to Die: The Battle of Stones River.* Urbana: University of Illinois Press, 1990.

_____. *This Terrible Sound: The Battle of Chickamauga.* Urbana: University of Illinois Press, 1992.

Dyer, Frederick H. *A Compendium of the War of the Rebellion.* 3 vols. New York: Thomas Yoseloff, 1959.

Evans, Clement, ed. *Confederate Military History: A Library of Confederate States History.* Vol. 10, *Louisiana and Arkansas.* Atlanta: Confederate Publishing Company, 1899.

Foote, Shelby. *The Civil War: A Narrative.* 3 vols. New York: Random House, 1958-74.

Freeman, Douglas Southall. *Lee's Lieutenants: A Study in Command.* 3 vols. New York: Charles Scribner's Sons, 1942-44.

Frohman, Charles E. *Rebels on Lake Erie: The Piracy, the Conspiracy, Prison Life.* Columbus: Ohio Historical Society, 1965.

Glaser, Lena Jo Kelly. *Hufstedler Family and Allied Families.* Philadelphia: Xerox Reproduction Center, 1974.

Harshman, Linda Flint. compl. *Index to the 1860 Federal Population Census of Ohio.* Vol. 1. Ann Arbor, MI: Edward Bros., Inc., 1979.

Hays, Elinor Rice. *Morning Star: A Biography of Lucy Stone, 1818-1893.* New York: Harcourt, Brace & World, 1961.

Hibben, Paxton. *Henry Ward Beecher: An American Portrait.* New York: The Press of the Readers Club, 1942.

Ingmire, Francis T. compl. *Arkansas Confederate Veterans and Widows Pension Applications.* St.Louis: Francis T. Ingmire, 1985.

Johnson, Ludwell H. *Red River Campaign: Politics and Cotton in the Civil War.* 2nd ed. Kent, OH: Kent State University Press, 1993.

Killgore, Nettie Hicks. *History of Columbia County, Arkansas.* Magnolia, AR: Magnolia Printing Co., 1947.

Knight, Rena Marie. compl. *Confederate Soldiers Buried in Arkansas.* Jacksonville, AR: R.M.K. Publishing Co., 1999.

Lee, Alfred E. *History of the City of Columbus: Capitol of Ohio.* 2 vols. New York: Munsell & Co., 1892.

McLane, Bobbie Jones and Desmond Walls Allen. *Arkansas 1850 Census Every-Name Index.* Conway, AR: Arkansas Research, 1995.

McPherson, James M. *Battle Cry of Freedom: The Civil War Era.* New York: Oxford University Press, 1988.

_____. *The Struggle for Equality: Abolitionists and the Negro in the Civil War and Reconstruction.* Princeton, NJ: Princeton University Press, 1964.

Miller, Francis Trevelyan, ed. *Photographic History of the Civil War.* 10 vols. New York: The Review of Reviews Co., 1912.

Mueller, Myrl Rhine. "Is it Pruet or Pruett?." *Greene County Historical Quarterly* 4 (Summer 1968), 15-16.

Nevins, Allan. *The War for the Union.* 4 vols. New York: Charles Scribner's Sons, 1959-71.

_____. *Fremont: Pathmarker of the West.* New York: Appleton Century Company, 1939.

Osborne, Charles C. *Jubal: The Life and Times of General Jubal A. Early, CSA.* Chapel Hill, NC: Algonquin Books of Chapel Hill, 1992.

Pulaski County, Arkansas Marriage Record Index, 1820-1901. Conway, AR: Arkansas Research, 2000.

Sifakis, Stewart. *Compendium of the Confederate Armies: Alabama.* New York: Facts on File, 1992.

_____. *Compendium of the Confederate Armies: Florida and Arkansas.* New York: Facts on File, 1992.

Stevenson, Alexander F. *The Battle of Stone's River Near Murfreesboro, Tenn., December 30, 1862 To January 3, 1863.* Boston: James R. Osgood and Company, 1884.

Sword, Wiley. *Embrace an Angry Wind: The Confederacy's Last Hurrah: Spring Hill, Franklin, and Nashville.* New York: HarperCollins Publishers, 1992.

Symonds, Craig L. *Stonewall of the West: Patrick Cleburne & The Civil War.* Lawrence: University of Kansas Press, 1997.

Warner, Ezra J. *Generals in Gray: Lives of the Confederate Commanders.* Baton Rouge: Louisiana State University Press, 1995.

Wert, Jeffry. *From Winchester to Cedar Creek: The Shenandoah Campaign of 1864.* Mechanicsburg, PA: Stackpole Books, 1997.

Wigginton, Thomas A. et al. *Tennesseans in the Civil War: A Military History of Confederate and Union Units with Available Rosters of Personnel.* 2 vols. Nashville: Civil War Centennial Commission, 1964.

Wills, Brian Steel. *A Battle from the Start: The Life of Nathan Bedford Forrest.* New York: HarperCollins Publishers, Inc., 1992.

Wilson, W. Emerson. *Fort Delaware.* Newark: University of Delaware Press, 1957.

About the Editor

Brian K. Robertson is a graduate of the University of Central Arkansas with a bachelors degree in history. He is currently employed as the Manuscripts Coordinator at the Butler Center for Arkansas Studies at the Central Arkansas Library System, Little Rock.